The Beginner's Guide
to Show Jumping

THE BEGINNER'S GUIDE TO Show Jumping

Peter Churchill

BLANDFORD PRESS
POOLE   DORSET

First published in the UK 1982 by Blandford Press,
Link House, West Street, Poole, Dorset, BH15 1LL

Copyright © 1982 Blandford Books Ltd

British Library Cataloguing in Publication Data

Churchill, Peter
 The beginner's guide to show jumping.
 1. Show jumping
 I. Title
 798.2'5   SF295.5

ISBN 0 7137 1096 9

All rights reserved. No part of this book may be reproduced or transmitted in any form or by any means, electronic or mechanical, including photocopying, recording or any information storage and retrieval system, without permission in writing from the Publisher.

Typeset by Permanent Typesetting & Printing Co. Ltd., Hong Kong.

Printed by Butler & Tanner Ltd., Frome, Somerset.

Contents

1	Introduction — The Basics	7
2	The Right Pony	13
3	The Training Area and Equipment	25
4	Fitness and Ground-work	35
5	The Lunge-Rein and Practice Fences	59
6	Practice Makes Perfect	81
7	Preparing for the Show	95
8	The Care of Equipment	105
	Glossary	113
	Simplified Rules of Show Jumping	115
	Useful Addresses	116
	Acknowledgements	117
	Index	119

1 Introduction

The Basics

An Olympic show jumping gold medallist once told me, 'If there is a secret to the game, it's getting the right instructor at the very beginning of your career, and as for the horse it's the level of the handling he has experienced *before* he starts jumping training that counts.' Now these are two important points. First, getting the right instructor means not necessarily the most celebrated, but the right one for you. This is the instructor whom you like, you feel you can work with and you feel has the professional ability and experience to bring you through each phase of your career at just the right time. Second, the standard of the horse's training on the flat will determine not only how good a show jumper he is going to be, but also how consistent a performer he will be in the show ring.

Riding is a sport that demands a certain amount of physical dexterity, application and fitness, although perhaps not to the level demanded of the athlete. But show jumping is an athletic activity for both horse and rider; fitness, training and competitive instinct become the prime factors which will make the difference between success and failure.

Why theorize about a sport? Well, I suppose the answer to that is that ability in a sport tends to progress from the basic level the more you get involved, and the more you get involved the better you want to do it. Show jumping is a good example of this for most competitors start out not too seriously at Pony Club/Riding Club level, or at unaffiliated shows, but before very long they are setting their sights on qualifying for one of the big junior championships at a major national show.

So let us start from the basis that the better we play a game (in other words, the more correct our techniques and attitudes), the more exciting and satisfying the results will be. But before we start to build on this foundation, we must decide what type of competitor we are going to be, for, as in most things in life, there is more than one way of approaching show jumping as a competitive game. Basically, there are only two schools of thought. For the sake of clarity let us call these two schools, the *physical rider* and the *technical rider*.

The physical rider relies on his dominance of the horse as a vehicle to achieve the rider's aims, i.e. to win a competition, with complete disregard for the style, technique or manner in which it is done. These riders, many of them very gifted in their own way, are what international team coaches call 'flair' riders. They have great competitive spirit, a talent for split-second timing and the gymnastic ability to give their horses freedom in the air over a fence while exerting the maximum pressures and control of their horses on the flat. They 'over-ride' their horses never letting the animal think for itself, or shine as an athlete. We are not discussing here whether any particular system is wrong or right for, in any competitive sport, it is often the results that count in the end. The 'flair' riders certainly get results but they are often inconsistent and their horses are usually 'burned-out' very early in their careers. The *physical school* follows a simple system; given the strength and gymnastic suppleness it is not difficult to influence the mind and body of a domesticated animal, but the system produces its own drawbacks. The results, although sometimes brilliant, tend to be inconsistent and the 'wear and tear' on the animal has the influence of shortening its career. This domination of the animal is more apparent in junior jumping as most trainers are too big or too heavy to be able to school ponies under saddle and artificial methods, such as severe bits or tight martingales, have to be used to aid a young rider lacking in experience, ability or strength. Now we will be discussing in this book the training of a pony and rider for competitive jumping but, although there are some minor differences, the principles of training and schooling can be equally as effective in the production of a young show jumping horse.

The technical rider, or let us call it the *technical school*, follows a graduated schooling programme which has as its base the aim of educating the pony to its job, whether it be show jumping or any other horse-sport discipline, with the minimum and simplest forms of intervention by the rider. Where the physical school tends to 'over-ride' their ponies the technical school tends to 'under-ride' them, leaving the animals to use their natural abilities as athletes, their flair and power. Now all systems have their advantages and disadvantages. The drawback of what we are defining as the technical school system is that longer must be spent on the basic schooling of the pony through its flat-work. Attention to detail must be given to feeding programmes to produce muscle, while keeping the pony mentally calm, and the pony must be obtained young.

The benefits of the system are consistent results and performances once the pony has gained show experience and very little 'wear and tear' on the pony, physically or mentally. Anyone taking on the pony after you will get nothing but joy from sitting on his back. In other words, you will always have the option of attracting a prospective purchaser if your pony is correctly schooled, making it a relatively easy ride for any other experienced and correctly trained child rider. This advantage is always worth bearing in mind for young riders can, sometimes almost overnight, completely outgrow a certain size pony, or find themselves out of the age group division permitted to ride a pony of certain measurements. So a good pony that you have outgrown can and will be of tremendous use to someone else, thus giving him a certain market value according to his ability and track-record. What must be remembered is that unless the rider is very good, with a strong competitive spirit, and the pony has a natural physical aptitude for gymnastic and athletic performances, no system will take the rider or the pony to the top. The rider should certainly strive to use correct and polished techniques but following a pattern or doctrine is not enough in itself, the rider must want to jump and win. The pony must be trained and schooled to a physical and mental peak but, again, that will not be enough unless the pony likes jumping and is full of courage. Only in the best possible world will a novice pony jumper move through a training and schooling programme without placing a foot wrong at least once. As the father of World and European Champion David Broome, Fred senior, told me, 'We should only train our horses up to 80% and leave 20% to the horse. Even the best riders get into trouble at least once in a round...and when this happens it is that 20% 'horse' which helps them out. It is only the very good, thinking horse that can get out of trouble. That's what makes good jumping horses.'

Sometimes in competition riding, style, elegance and technique has to take a back seat and it's 'heads down let's go boys'.

There can be fewer more satisfying sights than an educated, physically fit pony jumping fences willingly and gracefully. Show jumping is one of the clearest expressions of the sport of riding and the success of completing a course of show fences, laid out and designed by someone else, with style, technique and fluency is just as good a proof of horsemanship as a mantle-shelf smothered in cups, medals and ribbons. If the initial aims of the preliminary training programme are achieved, i.e. a calm, educated pony with a supple, technically correct rider, then the red ribbons will not be all that far away.

The horse and pony are not by nature jumping animals. When left to themselves the majority of horses and ponies will show no inclination and very little aptitude for leaping over any object that may cross their path or restrict their freedom. The only occasions when they will attempt jumping is when fleeing danger, or through panic, but even then very few horses or ponies will manage even the simplest of obstacles. Many experiments have been carried out to test and explain this difference between 'natural' behaviour and 'trained' behaviour. An especially interesting one was set up in the USA a few years ago when a group of horses, young, old, trained and untrained, were left in a paddock with poor pasture on one side of a small fence of rails, with a paddock of good pasture on the other. It was found that over 90% of the group remained in the poor pasture paddock, while those that did jump over to the better, pasture were all trained horses.

Jumping is a gymnastic exercise and the pony does need to be educated to it. The pony's body must be fit and supple and his mind relaxed. He must be taught to jump willingly and obediently. Ponies, I have found, tend to have a better aptitude for jumping than horses. However, we must remember that in show jumping we are asking the unnatural in so much as the pony must jump on his own in the ring and he must clear the fences. The student rider has to undergo similar training in many ways in that he, or she, must be fit and supple, with a relaxed mental attitude and a riding standard that in no way hinders or unbalances the pony.

To sum up, the pony is not a 'natural' jumper, in the correct meaning of the term, but he can develop into a powerful and efficient athlete. The rider's job is both a physical and mental one; his movements and actions are at all times directly relevant to the athletic ability and natural grace of the pony.

2 The Right Pony

Before we can discuss the ideal physical characteristics of the jumping pony, we must first of all study the mechanics of the animal's body when jumping a show fence. For the purpose of show jumping we are looking for certain vital points in the pony's physical form that may not be so important, or even needed, in the pony that is required for showing or cross-country jumping.

The first thing to remember is that unlike other forms of riding where jumping is involved, e.g. hunting, point-to-pointing, steeplechasing, eventing and team cross-country riding, show jumping has to be performed 'cold'. This means the pony does not have the incentive of herd-instinct which a horse has in racing over fences, or the advantage of using speed to make the height or length of an obstacle as in cross-country riding. So the animal must be capable of performing on his own, under widely varying conditions, over all kinds of different fences, and at varying paces according to

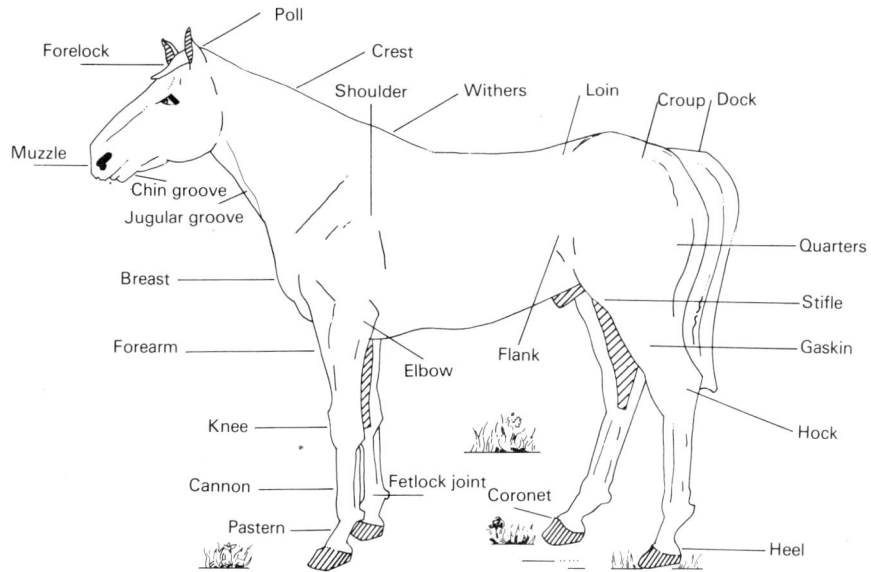

Fig. 1 The points of the pony.

13

different classes and conditions, i.e. whether it is the preliminary round or a jump-off against the clock. While physical make-up is important, as this helps balance, temperament and aptitude for intensive athletic and gymnastic training is, therefore, just as essential for the show jumping pony. This means what is in the 'heart', the personality and character of the pony, should be considered as much as the perfect lines of the body.

Muscular power and a free-flowing movement are the essence of the jumping-pony's technique. The activity and strength of the hindquarters and hindlegs are the source of the 'lift'. (Often mistakenly defined as the 'spring'). An easy striding action is the basis of the jumping pony's equilibrium. Sound legs are essential for support in take-off and for accepting the shock of landing. The pony, unlike the cat or dog (animals with natural spring) does not have soft feet or padded paws to act as shock absorbers, thus the strain on his limbs, particularly the lower regions, is considerable. Good round feet are needed, with plenty of interior space for protection as the weight of pony and rider come to ground on the landing side. The head and neck form the balancing pole and the back is both a support and an extension of this balance.

The trained jumper should jump out of his stride, which means he should not have to be *forced* back onto his hindquarters in order to go into the air and over a fence. On the approach to a fence the pony lowers his head and stretches his neck. What he is doing is looking for the ground-line or base-line of the obstacle so that he can calculate its height. In doing this he can balance himself and prepare his hocks (hindlegs) for the take-off. The pony cannot rely on 'spring' in the true sense of the word. He gets his elevation from the pushing power of his hocks, so he engages his 'engine' to get lift-off.

On arriving at the point of take-off, the pony shortens his neck and brings his hocks well under his body. The hocks then take the strain and lift the forehand up and into the air. As he does so the pony folds up his front legs and stretches the head and neck out from his shoulders. Once in the air, the period of suspension above the fence, the pony has his head and neck extended to the maximum in a downward attitude. It is this downward stretch, or extension of the neck and head, that helps the pony through his back to raise his hindquarters and 'throw' his hindlegs up and away from him to clear the fence.

As he lands the pony reaches forward with the forelegs to take the shock of landing, raising the head and shortening the neck to prepare his hindquarters to come down underneath him for the first full stride on landing.

With these points in mind, what are we looking for in the perfectly made jumping-pony? Well, let us take a close look at the working parts of our jumper.

The Feet These should be round and large enough to support the pony's body weight. Small feet, for example, on a large pony, or big feet on a light pony, will make him difficult to train. The sole of the foot must be slightly but definitely concave. This will give the pony a better foothold. The frog should be well defined and rubber-like to touch.

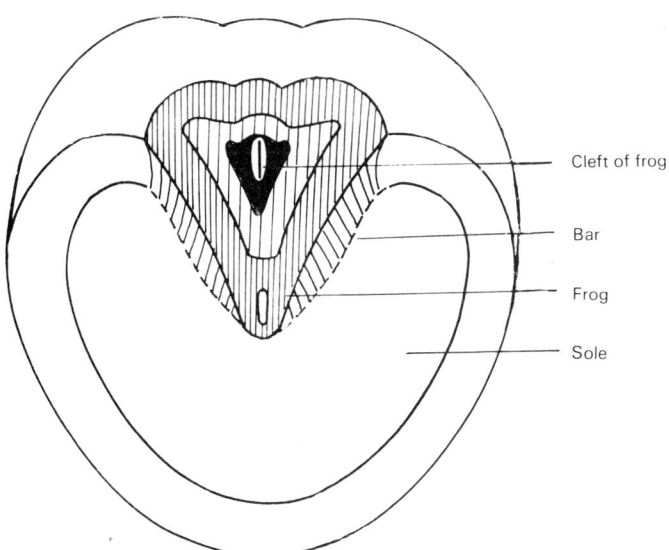

Fig. 2 The foot. One of the most important considerations in producing competition horses and ponies is care of the feet. They must have regular attention from the farrier; they must be kept clean and the animal's bedding material should be fresh and dry at all times. 'No foot, no horse', may be a hackneyed old phrase but it says it all.

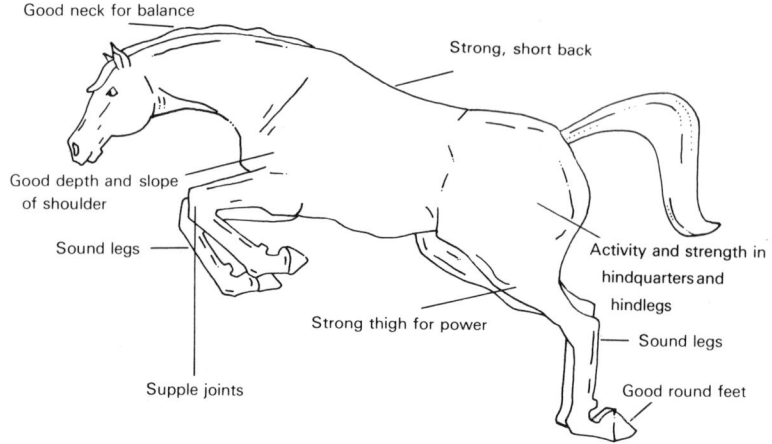

Fig. 3 The assets of the jumping pony.

The Pastern This should be long, well sloped and strong looking. Too straight a pastern, or too short a one, will hinder the stride of the pony in the extended and shortened gaits. We will later see that the ability to change 'gear' from one length of stride to another is absolutely vital to the jumping pony.

The Cannon and Tendons These should be short and strong as they take most of the strain in jumping. If the cannon and tendon are too long, or too finely boned, they will not stand up to intensive training, let alone the pounding they will have to take in the competition arena.

The Knees and Hocks The knee joints and the hock joints should be large, bony and flat. These form the vital hinges in the pony's jumping technique, so the larger and flatter they are the more flexible and efficient they will be.

The Forearm and Shoulder The forearm should be set well into the breast and shoulders with a pronounced muscular shape, rather like the developed biceps of a human athlete. The shoulder should be flat rather than fleshy, sloping well back to the wither to give the maximum pendulum action, making the lengthening and shortening of strides graceful and easy.

Chest and Girth The chest must be deep when looked at from the front and from the side. The broad-based, deep chest will show the amount of heart room the pony has as an athlete. The heart pumps blood around the body at varying rates. During periods of rest the rate is slower than when approaching a show fence or, indeed, when jumping a treble combination, or in a jump-off against the clock. In other words, at times of maximum effort the heart rate is at its fastest. The heart expands and contracts to pump blood around the body and the larger the chest cavity the more easily it can reach maximum expansion. One large expansion, followed by a maximum contraction, puts less strain on the heart's pumping function than several short expansions followed by quick short contractions. So having a deep line through the girth is not enough for a performance pony. Depth alone will not give heart space, it must be accompanied by width.

The width of the chest must not be so exaggerated as to appear heavy or clumsy, otherwise that is exactly what the pony will be in its jumping technique. Also, the depth and width of the chest and girth must be in proportion. The lungs, like the heart, are at their simplest a pumping apparatus for the processing of air. Again, in a narrow pony the lungs will be restricted. So the barrel of the body and the rib-cage must be well rounded, tapering into the loin and hip areas. A short back is better than a long back in the jumping pony, for obvious reasons. (One good way of judging the back is to imagine the pony ridden.) The back should be short enough for the rider and saddle to fit comfortably into the middle of the back with very little 'left over' between the back of the saddle and the pony's hip-joint. A pony that is too long in the back will be difficult to train as true balance will rarely be achieved and, what is more important perhaps, it will be very difficult to get into really tip-top condition.

The rib-cage should be well sprung and come right up to the hip-joint. The wither bone should be well defined so that the saddle settles securely in the correct area of the back.

The Tail This is often overlooked, in my opinion, in studies of conformation. It is an extension of the spine and back so its position and the way the pony carries it is, I think, quite a vital clue as to how the

A good example of a 12 hh jumping pony. Strong, well-balanced, and with a good 'front', this pony will give a child rider confidence and security.

pony will use his back when jumping. Although the pony cannot bend his spine in the true sense we do require him to 'bend' or 'tip' over the top of a show fence. Senior international rider, Freddie Welch, puts it more graphically, I think, when he says, 'I like to see a jumper pour over his fence, like milk coming out of a jug.' So I like to see a tail set high and carried with pride. A pony that flags his tail tends to be supple in his back muscles, whereas a pony that tucks his tail in tends to be stiff in his back.

The Neck and Head The neck should be long, taper into the head and not be set low into the shoulders and breast area. A good neck and front is what is known as 'plenty of rein'. Such a pony will be easier to bridle and school, having natural balance from his length of rein, whereas a pony that is short or thick of neck will have balance problems when ridden, and the rider will have bridle problems in

The child's ideal all-round competition pony — well-made, strong and with that Welsh-blood 'front'. This 13 hh gelding trained on to compete very successfully in working hunter pony classes, dressage and show jumping.

jumping schooling. Similarly, if a pony is too light of neck he will tend, through lack of strength in this area, to 'overbend' to his bridle. If the neck is the pony's balancing pole, its length and depth must be relative to the length and depth of the pony's body.

Bold, large ears are said to denote a generous nature and nine and half times out of ten this old yardstick is right. A nice head should be broad at the top, tapering to the nose, with well-rounded nostrils. The pony's eyes should be set low in the head, large and wide apart.

Buying the Jumping Pony

Time is money in show jumping, as in all things. If you cannot put in the time, but still want success, you will have to put in the money. There are two ways of approaching a career in competitive show

Graham Fletcher riding the Irish-bred Preachan. Graham was a member of the Bedale Branch of the Pony Club and competed in one day events. His first jumping pony was Ivy Dene.

jumping: either you can buy a young pony and train it up the grades yourself, or you can buy an experienced animal which is already in, or near, the open grade. Now, obviously the second method is going to cost quite a lot of money, and the first method is going to demand a considerable amount of time. So these two factors — time and/or money — are the first that must be evaluated.

Weighing up the factors involved is best done by the student's riding coach and parents. The coach will know which type of pony will be suitable and be able to assess the pupil's ability to produce (or not to produce) his or her own open pony. The parents, obviously, will know how much can or cannot be spent on the project. So when, or what, to buy can be judged by these people, but the next question is where to buy. This can be a difficult one to answer.

Whether you are a junior rider or a young adult rider starting out you may decide to follow the 'schoolmaster' system. That is to buy an experienced pony or horse that will safely introduce you to show jumping rather than vice versa. The best way to approach this is to travel the show circuit and watch the top junior competitions. Many top jumping ponies pass from family to family over a considerable number of years. Jumping ponies tend to have a much longer competitive life than horses. As one rider grows too big or becomes too old to ride within a certain age-group classification the owners put the pony up for sale. So watch the ponies ridden by 15- and 16-year-olds who are in their second-last or very last season of junior jumping. If you see one you like, and that your coach thinks you will be able to ride, then your parents can approach the owners and often arrange to buy the pony at the end of the season. But of course these ponies are worth a considerable amount of money, so this is certainly not a cheap route into competition riding. In all fairness, it is not a short route either for these experienced ponies often take a lot of riding and are nine times out of ten too old to change their ways. The rider must adapt to the pony which is not always as easy as it sounds.

Let us assume then that you decide to go for the novice pony with the intention of producing him through the grades. For the experienced child or young rider, that is a rider who has been

Pam Dunning on the New Zealand-bred Roscoe. Pam is one of Europe's most successful show jumping riders. Before taking up show jumping seriously she was a leading point-to-point rider.

correctly trained and given some sound experience in pony club competitions, the younger, better bred pony is the best buy, providing it has had sound basic training — in other words it has been correctly 'broken-in' and been given elementary schooling on the flat as well as over small obstacles. Breeding is your guide here; the blood-line can tell you everything. Look for the pony, or young horse, with papers that prove how and when it was bred. In the stallion look for quality; in the brood-mare look for some jumping form or success in working hunter pony classes. Mares will often pass on to their progeny jumping aptitude, while stallions will tend to pass on their conformation and sometimes their ability as well.

For the 10 to 15-year-old child the best type of jumping pony is one of the native breeds, or a native cross-bred such as the Connemara, or Welsh, or the Welsh crossed with Arab or Thoroughbred blood. For the 10 to 11-year-old child it is best to start with a pony standing at 12.2 hh, or just under 13.2 hh, working up to the 14.2 hh pony for the older child. In the case of the young adult rider a thoroughbred-cross-bred animal, or an Anglo-Arab is usually the better buy for serious competition work, rather than the pure thoroughbred which can often be just that little bit too much for many riders. But the thoroughbred crossed with the Welsh Cob or the Cleveland Bay usually produces an animal with the right conformation and aptitude for competition jumping.

The best advice any book can give on this delicate and often complicated area is to be guided by your coach or a recognized expert (as against a self-appointed one!) and have the pony, or horse, thoroughly examined by a veterinarian, including the X-raying of all four feet and lower legs.

3 The Training Area and Equipment

No matter for what purpose the pony is going to be used, whether as a jumper, show pony or just for pleasure, some form of dressage training must be given so that the pony will carry himself and his rider in a balanced and comfortable manner.

Dressage can mean different things to different people. To some it is a form of competition, to others almost a circus act and to a third group a closed book. But to the future jumping pony basic dressage training is essential because the domesticated equine cannot develop along the same lines as his wild brother. Man and his horse-management are responsible for his growth and development not nature. So dressage comes in as a substitute for nature by bringing the horse systematically to physical and mental maturity.

The pony is a creature of the open-air so, no matter how intensive our competition training programme may be, we should never forget the pony's natural spirit and dignity. It is most important that we do not put him in situations which will destroy these qualities.

First of all we must define the word dressage in relation to the training of the show jumper. Dressage with this in mind simply means obedience and suppleness so all the work on the flat must be designed to make the jumper firstly, a good willing ride and secondly, an efficient athlete. So what determines whether or not a pony is a good ride? First and foremost we must ride the pony in such a way that he does not find the experience uncomfortable or unpleasant. Now the pony has very little choice in the matter so it is up to us to show the animal that the better he carries himself the easier his job is going to be. Good ponies make good riders; good riders make good ponies better; but bad riding makes bad horses. It is as simple as that. So now we can list what makes a pony a good ride and an efficient athlete:

1. The pony should go forward freely, and with a balanced rhythm.
2. The pony must have a steady head carriage.
3. The pony must be balanced in all gaits.
4. The pony must move 'straight'.
5. The pony must be supple, and confident of its physical ability.
6. The pony must willingly obey the rider's aids.

These are the stages we must work through in linking the work on the flat to jumping training. But before we can start seriously on this work we must first look at the facilities we will need and the equipment we will use.

The Training Area

Jumping education is intensive training so we will need a manege, a defined training area. This can be a flat, well-sheltered area, measuring some 46 × 18 metres (150 × 60 ft), which is well drained. But that is not as easy as it may sound for if the surface is grass it will only be available in certain types of weather conditions. If it gets too wet, no matter how well drained it might be, the surface is going to get poached and uneven, and if it gets too dry the surface is going to get too hard. So the answer to all these disadvantages is an all-weather schooling arena. There are several

The training area needs looking after every day. A good jumping surface for young horses and ponies will encourage efficient performances, but a poor, uneven surface will encourage carelessness.

ways this can be achieved, (a) have an all-weather arena of wood-bark or tan, laid down by a specialist firm, or (b) make your own with the help of a local landscaper.

If an indoor riding hall is possible so much the better, for here pony and rider can work unhindered under consistent conditions. Both the all-weather ring and the indoor arena are the gymnasiums of jumping training. In these the really concentrated work is done to bring the pony to his peak as a jumper. However, one must always keep in mind that variety is the spice of life. We want the jumping pony to be 100% obedient but what we do not want is a brain-washed jumping machine, so mix up the daily work between sessions in the 'gymnasium' and long relaxed walks around your own paddock, or paddocks, or that of a neighbouring farmer. Nowadays a quiet ride around the roads and lanes is no longer on, in

Long, relaxed walks are good for fitness and make a break from the intensive routine of training. Under the right conditions it is good for the rider to ride-out bareback and it helps to relax the pony.

my opinion, for even with the most traffic-proof pony I think the risks are too great. Most farmers will let you *walk* around the edges of their fields and I do mean *walking only*, there is no need for the show jumper, pony or horse, to be galloped. His intensive work will keep him perfectly fit so riding-out sessions should be straight forward relaxation days...that means walking. If you are not able to avail yourself of fields for riding-out then, say, two days a week lunge your pony only and then turn him loose in the indoor school, a paddock or, if it is fenced properly, in the all-weather arena. The aim of practice fences is threefold: to improve the pony's style, confidence and technique over fences; to improve the rider's style, confidence and technique; and to prepare both pony and rider for the competition arena. The fences must therefore be designed and laid out to achieve these objects. Whether you make your own fences or buy a set of schooling fences will depend on how much you wish to spend, but the following points should be observed:

1. Variety is the most important factor and this can be achieved by working on the two basic types of show fence, vertical and spread, using different materials. For example, brush fences or oil drums make a vertical but placed in front of rails they make a spread; one can also make a gate, some ditches, and double and treble combinations. Try to use rustic rails as well as coloured rails.

2. Again, for variety, do not site the fences in a circle or uniform lay-out but try to position them so there are at least two changes of rein, and plan at least two fences that can be jumped in both directions.

3. You should always have somebody working with you 'on the ground', either your riding coach or a parent, during all schooling sessions over fences.

4. The type of ground you put your practice fences on is just as important as the siting of them. The 'going' or 'footing' (the state of the ground) must be the best possible. Heavy (wet or sticky) going could frighten a young pony or, worse still for a show jumper, make him careless in his jumping. Equally, ground that is too hard can cause leg and muscular problems. So move your practice fences

One way to give the schooling fences a different look without frightening the pony. (The water troughs were from the calf-pens, the trees in tubs from the terrace, and the straw bales from the barn.) But, whatever you use, ask father first!

regularly (unless, of course, you have them in an all-weather arena). Jumping ponies tend to poach the landing and take-off areas at fences when working on grass.

5. The pony tends to measure his fences and distances from ground level upwards. So make the base-lines of your practice fences absolutely clear. For example, place a coloured rail underneath a vertical on the ground, or in front of a spread, or some small painted oil drums or barrels.

6. It is of more value in schooling to arrange your practice fences so that the spreads can easily be opened-up and made wider. This is more important than the heights in many ways because increasing spreads, before increasing heights, will encourage the pony to use his body well and encourage the rider to 'go with the movement' more.

7. Try to make the practice fences as inviting as possible by keeping the poles clean and by avoiding split or chipped rails. Make the wings look like part of the fence giving it plenty of width.

8. Have some fences that can be seen through, but not to the point of being flimsy.

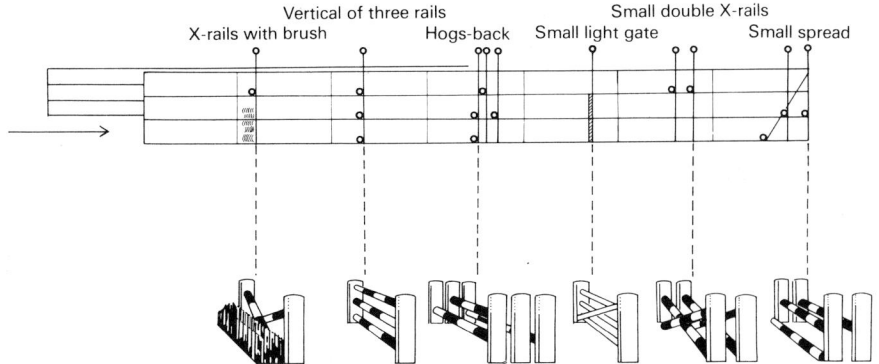

Fig. 4 The jumping lane, or chute. The fences, which ideally should number about six or seven, must be low, with a mixture of verticals and spreads.

Fig. 5 The jumping box is useful in practising control and approaches.

If you have the space, a jumping lane is well worth having for work under saddle, loose or on the lunge. It should be sited in a wind-protected area, preferably with a natural enclosure along one side such as a thick hedge, high wall or bank, and the 'open' side should be enclosed by a high post and rail barrier. The fences, which ideally should number about six or seven, must be low, natural-looking and with a mixture of verticals and spreads. Included in the lane can be a grid of low fences set at a distance of one stride between each, while the other fences should be set on several even strides. (*Fig. 4*). Again, allow for drainage and keep out of the lane in wet weather.

Equipment

So much then for facilities, now we must put together some specialized equipment before starting work in earnest. All the equipment used in jumping training is chosen or designed to improve the pony's technique and athletic qualities. When working young ponies I like to have them in 'boots', or bandages, to protect their front legs and, depending on the pony's action, also in 'brushing boots' and 'over-reach boots'. Additionally, when working young horses (ponies, I find, tend to be more clever than horses) I like to have a pair of knee-guards on them, certainly at the lungeing stage of their training.

The object of the preliminary training programme will be to teach the pony to carry himself with balance and a steady rhythm. To

The draw-rein and the jumping boots are fitted. Fortunately, this pony is so clean and positive in his movement that he has never needed brushing boots or over-reach boots. This is often the case with small ponies but those of 14.2 hh, and horses, often need just a bit more protection from their own feet.

achieve this end we will be using elastic side-reins and draw-reins. Neither type, contrary to popular belief, can or do force the pony to carry his head and neck in a certain position. If used for that purpose they will have the negative effect of destroying the traction of the hindlegs and the obedience to bridle. (Both these factors are very necessary in show jumping.)

The elastic side-reins fitted to the saddle, or a roller, are used in lungeing work, both over small fences and poles on the ground, to encourage the pony to elevate his action, thus working the legs and joints, and to use his body to maintain balance while submitting to the bridle. So we gain two end results, muscle with suppleness and balance with smoothness.

The draw-rein, a simple piece of equipment that can be very dangerous in uneducated hands, or if used on a pony that is not ready for intensive training, helps the trainer to encourage the pony to submit to the bridle while building muscles on the neck and loins.

4 Fitness and Ground-work

There is a difference between work and exercise; a narrow one perhaps but nonetheless it exists and it is important. Basically it amounts to this — exercise is concerned with improving and hardening muscles, with keeping unwanted fat off the conditioned body while 'exercising' the lungs (wind) and the heart (circulation). Work is schooling (education) and preparation for a specific job through suppling, muscle formation, technique and calming the mind. All aspects must be directly related to the diet and the age of the pony. For example, bringing an experienced pony up to competition fitness will be easier than bringing a young novice pony to the same physical state.

Exercise

We will work to the principle that the object of exercise is to build and maintain condition. Exercising must be planned to build up progressively, starting off with a short period each day at a slow pace, plenty of active walking and slow trotting over a fairly flat terrain, with some 15 to 20 minutes relaxed walking to finish.

As the pony gets fitter so the exercise periods and their pace can be increased. You will be able to judge the pony's progress towards fitness by the rhythm of his breathing. As he gets 'harder' he will blow less and breathe with an effortless and even rhythm. The aim at the beginning is to work off naturally any fat the pony is carrying from his 'soft' condition. This is particularly difficult, if possible at all, with the grass-kept pony as he will not be getting enough protein to help him reach the required 'hard' condition. For this reason I never turn out our competition ponies, certainly not during the showing season, but in the afternoon we often lead them out to get some sun on their backs (when we can find it in Britain!) and to taste some nice sweet grass. But I think if you are aiming at show jumping seriously, in either the junior or senior division, you cannot risk turning your animals out to grass for any lengthy periods. Further, modern show jumping is now so competitive that your animals must be at their peak or near-peak for every public outing.

However, there are some ponies, particularly the very small ones, 12.2 hh, which might be better off spending at least half their day out on grass when conditions permit.

The 'hardening' process can only be done gradually as any stress or effort-demanding work undertaken when the pony is carrying too much fat can do irreparable damage to that pony's wind and heart.

It is almost impossible to lay down hard and fast rules or principles governing time and number of weeks needed to get a pony fit. Jumping ponies, like any other athlete, vary considerably in how much exercise they may need or how long it will take to get them fit and hard. Our grey pony, William, needs very little exercise and work to bring him to a hard and fit state, whereas our bay pony, Fiddler, needs weeks of slow work before he is even ready for serious schooling. The trouble with Fiddler is, like all the British native breeds, he can get fat just thinking about food! So a good measure of common sense is required in interpreting the following guide lines.

Each period of exercise must start with at least 15 minutes free walking and finish with at least 20 minutes of free walking. The initial period helps the pony to get any stiffness out of his limbs or joints, in other words it warms him up, while the returning walk helps him to relax after exercise and to 'cool-off' before going back to his stall or loose-box. These opening and closing periods are also the time when the rider should be attending to girths. When on the way out to exercise they should be tightened, and when on the way back, loosen them.

To begin with the exercise periods should be around 45 minutes per day, building up over a period to an hour, or an hour and a half. But if your pony needs more than this, and you will able to tell by his behaviour, then divide the exercise periods into two, for example, one in the morning and another in the afternoon. One day should be set aside as a day off for the pony; this gap in the programme is a useful time to give bran mashes etc., or for arranging attention from the farrier.

The aim must be to build up to steady exercise at a consistent pace and rhythm in the walk, trot and canter. The pony should be given as much freedom as possible, especially of his head and neck, and uphill and downhill work must be brought into the programme as soon as the pony is starting to show signs of fitness. Where we live there are no hills at all so we have built a long, high bank with earth taken from our levelling operations when building the barn and sand arena; we use this as a substitute for uphill and downhill work. Slow, regulated trotting uphill builds muscle, particularly in the hindquarters and over the loins, and in the forearm and thigh, while walking on as free a rein as possible. Downhill encourages balance and works the muscles of the shoulder, back and neck. Fast trotting or fast galloping is of no value whatsoever.

The exercise programme and the work programme should be co-ordinated with the dual intention of not only getting the pony (and rider!) fit but also of adding variety to the daily programme. For example, a long exercise period can be followed by a short work period and vice versa, or one day the exercise period can be missed out altogether and an intensive work period on the flat, or jumping, substituted, or both can be left out one day and the pony just quietly ridden-out. Although regularity is the basis of any athlete's preparation, boredom or staleness should be carefully avoided.

Training

The complimentary objects of work is to educate, render supple and prepare the pony mentally and physically for a specific type of competition. For example, the eventing pony would be worked to a dressage/endurance/jumping programme — suppling his body, learning new movements, improving his responses to the riders' aids, etc. A show jumping pony's work is orientated to improving his discipline on the flat and his technique in jumping.

The art of working a jumping pony is to find the happy medium between repetition, which is going to be necessary to educate the animal, and boredom. Although we require a jumper that is going to be obedient and willing, it is wrong and self-defeating to turn the pony into a machine. Remember what Fred Broome senior, one of the great show jumping trainers of our time, said (which I have quoted earlier), '...leave 20% 'horse'...' With a little intelligent thought, a balance can be found.

As long as the owner/rider can keep some sort of variety in the programme, no matter how small, the pony's spirit and gaiety will not be lost. The pony can be taught to think for himself without tampering with his natural pride and spirit. This is especially true of the competition pony; flair used intelligently is the secret ingredient of the truly good pony and represents the 20% we want him to contribute from his natural abilities. So work must be consistent with only slight variations on the basic theme.

What about getting and keeping the rider fit? This is a question many young riders and trainers seem to overlook — their own state of fitness. You will not do justice to a talented, well-conditioned pony unless you yourself are in good physical and mental shape. Try to play as many other sports as you can, like tennis, football, rugby or swimming, to keep you fit and sharp and, above all, watch your diet and mental state as well as your pony's. Don't attempt to ride a 'schooling' session if you are feeling tired, have a cold, or are worried about something like exam results; these factors will affect the evenness of your temper and one bad 'schooling' period can destroy the work of months.

Working on the flat

So much for getting the pony ready for jumping training, now we must start the serious work on the flat and link that directly to training over fences. The three aims of our ground-work schooling will be (a) balance (both pony and rider), (b) control and obedience (dressage) and (c) suppleness (pony and rider). Now I have listed a series of exercises which should satisfy these three aims.

Balance Here we must go back to your original equitation classes and take a longer look at *collection*, perhaps the most difficult and complicated aspect of competition riding, which pony and rider must understand, control, create and know. Without correct collection pony and rider will never show over fences with good consistent results. As one old trainer once told me, 'There are an awful lot of cowboys in junior and elementary jumping, but very few horsemen.'

Fig. 6 Simple collection. The shortened form — energy contained. Compare with the uncollected shape.

Fig. 7 Uncollected. The lengthened form. Relaxed.

To understand collection we can, to a certain degree, liken the pony to the motor-car. Two more different locomotive vehicles might be difficult to find but we can use the principle of the motor-car to give us a graphic example of the theory of collection.

When the gearbox of a car is in neutral and the accelerator is not touched, the power unit is producing practically no energy and the vehicle will move neither backwards nor forwards. But if the gearbox is engaged the power unit will produce energy according to the amount of accelerator used, and that energy will be controlled by the driver. When the pony is in a state of collection, his hindquarters (the engine) are 'engaged' for producing energy and the rider, by using his open or closed hand, his legs and seat, can control the degree to which that energy is used. The relaxed pony, like the car in neutral, is not in a state of collection, is producing little or no energy and his hindquarters are not engaged, in other words he is in neutral. (*Fig. 7*).

Collection is the concentration of the pony's energy when his body is in the shortened form on a light rein (but positive rein not a loose rein), when he has maximum control over his body and limbs through the extra activity of his hindlegs and is in a postion to respond immediately to his rider's aids. It is rather like the principle of the spring which is wound up to a shortened form to contain the energy force and then lengthened when that energy force is released. (*Fig. 6*).

The pony is driven from behind, the hindquarters are his engine and his forward movement is produced from behind the saddle. His forehand is his support and his head and neck are his balancing pole. To concentrate the energy (winding up the spring, if you like) the rider must encourage activity while controlling its output rate. This must be done in such a way that the rider does not allow his weight to hinder the pony's natural support, the forehand. As the ultimate desire is to ride the pony without putting excessive strain on his body and to maintain his natural balance, then the total weight of the rider must be evenly distributed in the middle. The energy of the hindlegs (often referred to in this context as simply the 'hocks') is created and encouraged by the squeezing of the rider's legs and the drive of his seat-bones — the two most vital aids when approaching a fence. This energy is then restricted by the closed hands on the reins (*not and never* by pulling!), until required, thereby forcing the contained energy into an elevated attitude instead of a forward or backward attitude. By shortening the form of the pony's body, creating energy, bringing this energy to an elevated output, and by releasing it or containing it at will, the rider has in effect lightened the whole body of the pony. The pony at liberty can command his body and action in this way according to what he wishes to do. The rider allows the pony to have maximum control over his limbs, without strain, while carrying the weight of a rider.

Collection, briefly, is bringing the pony into a shortened form, which is essential to his preparation. This is achieved by the rider creating energy and controlling the rate of output of that energy.

Rhythm We can only achieve true balance by riding out of the pony all resistance in his body to the rider and the rider's aids. Later we will be discussing practising obedience to the rider's leg and seat aids, but first we must achieve willing obedience by the pony to his bridle. There is an old saying, 'No foot, no horse' and we can add to that for show jumping, 'No mouth, no jumper'. In other words, there is no way we can train a pony to jump a course of unnatural fences accurately and cleanly, with consistency, if the pony resists his bridle.

The lightness of the pony in our rein-hands is directly related to balance, but this overlaps with obedience. We achieve this lightness in hand by educating the pony to relax his lower jaw and accept his bridle. By stiffening the lower jaw the pony can resist his bridle and become heavy in the rider's hands. The negativeness of that, I think, is self-explanatory.

When a pony is in his natural state, perhaps in a field grazing, he has two ways of using his body when he wants to move. He can lengthen it for long strides or he can shorten it for short strides. It is this natural ability, this precise ability, that we require in the jumping pony *but* at our command and not his. Why? Simply because we walk the course before competing in a jumping class but the pony does not. So the pony does not know whether he is facing a vertical fence, a spread fence, a combination of fences, a short turn or a turn-back. Mind you I have seen some seasoned ponies and international show jumpers that 'suss-out' what sort of fences they are facing some three strides before their jockeys do!

To return to the day-to-day realities of the sport, if we are going to communicate with the animal through putting a lump of steel or what-have-you into an extremely sensitive part of his body, then we must do it in such a way that he understands without discomfort. So we work to get the pony to accept the bit in his mouth as naturally as possible, then we can take advantage of his natural ability to shorten or lengthen.

The work under saddle can begin once we see signs of the pony 'carrying himself' through his paces with no resistance to the bridle.

Throughout this phase of the training I use draw-reins. (*Page 32*). I have two main reasons for this, firstly, they encourage and help the pony to submit to his bridle without damaging his mouth or forcing him into an unnatural position and, secondly, they give the young rider complete control over the pony, thus building up in the pony's mind a healthy respect for the rider's commands. But, as with all artificial aids, there are hidden drawbacks and advantages; this is where the intelligence and knowledge of the coach is going to play a vital role. If the rider is allowed to ride on the draw-rein only, the pony will overbend to his bridle, in other words over-give to the bit, and this will have a tendency to lighten and shorten the strides of the hindlegs, a totally negative effect to the one we are looking for. For as we know by now the hind-end is where all the action should be — it is the engine. So the young rider must be carefully monitored so that he or she is constantly using the leg and seat aids to encourage active traction from the hindlegs all the time. One of the hidden advantages is that when used properly the draw-reins encourage muscle of the neck, shoulders, back and hindquarters. You will see in the photographs that I have my daughter riding in small, blunt spurs, so that her leg aids can be subtle and effective, keeping her out of the terrible 'kick and thump' technique one sees so much of in junior show jumping.

Every pony has a special kind of rhythm in his movement which is his natural and most comfortable 'gear'. Now this natural 'gear' is what we have to find in the jumping pony as soon as we

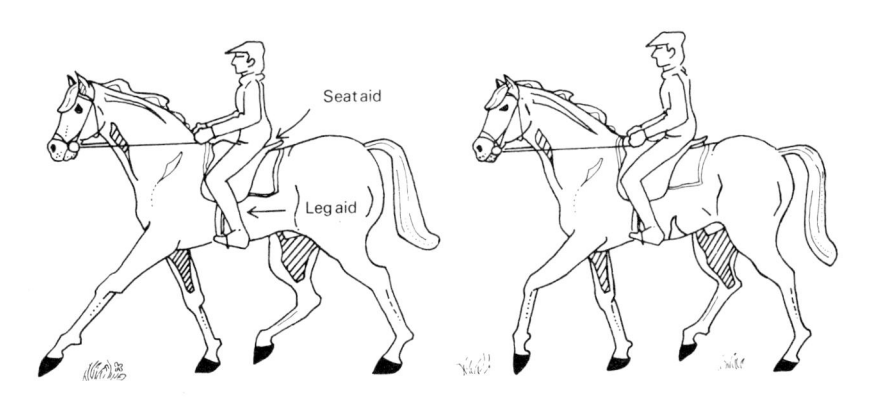

Fig. 8 Lengthening the stride by using the seat and leg aids and therefore encouraging the pony to maintain rhythm and pace in his strides.

can in the training programme, as this will be the best pace for him to come from when going for his fences. To find this 'gear', which exists in all paces, walk, trot and canter, is quite a simple process because the rider will feel the comfort and ease of the pace as the pony settles into it. Just letting the pony go charging along at, say, a fast trot is no good because the faster the pony's legs go the less control he, the pony, will have over his stride, and the rider's control over rhythm and balance will be negligible. Whereas, if the rider encourages the pony to keep a rhythmical, active trot, both pony and rider will have complete control over the pace.

One of the best illustrations of this work is at the trot but the principles for the canter are the same. The rider 'asks' the pony to trot with a brisk forward action on a regular one-two beat (in the canter, three beats). One beat for each diagonal movement (one diagonal being being near-fore and off-hind, and the other the off-fore with near-hind). The rider keeps a light but constant contact with the pony's mouth, using his leg aids to maintain the pace (leg on when the rider comes down in the saddle, and leg off when he rises; or in the sitting trot, leg on with one beat, leg off with the other beat), the rider must then concentrate on the length and rhythm of the stride. If the rider feels that the rhythm has changed, he 'asks' the pony to slow the pace, by closing his hands, squeezing with the leg aid, and pushing down into the saddle while keeping the leg aid

The transition from trot to canter. Study how the pony is using the power of his hindleg stride to 'raise' himself to the first stride of the canter, and how there is basically no change in the attitude and form of pony and rider. Particularly note the depth of the rider's seat and the light contact with the pony's mouth.

pressure on, then opening his fingers to allow the pony to trot on again at the balanced, even stride. If this is repeated each time the pony loses rhythm and evenness of stride, the pony will eventually, through self-demonstration as it were, settle into his 'gear' and hold it on an even, active stride. This groundwork is of paramount importance because with the show jumping pony we require the action to be 'active', we do not not want to waste energy. Along with this positive action we must have a 'cruising' stride, if you like, one that is even, powerful and balanced.

The following exercises and figures are the ones we recommend to attain the aims and objects we have been discussing while improving the pony's obedience, muscular development and gymnastic qualities. They should form an effective and intelligent basis to all groundwork needed for a show jumping pony, or horse.

Transitions As soon as the novice jumper is showing signs of moving at each pace with evenness and power, the serious work can be begun on making his transitions from one pace to another accurate and smooth. Unlike the schooling of the show pony where, perhaps, smoothness and grace can be more important in transitions, with the jumping pony we need above all else accuracy and balance. If we can attain style and grace as well, then the performance in the ring will be even better. But this will depend a great deal on the conformation and temperament of the pony and the natural ability of the rider. In other words, a pony which is a little too long in the back may not make a classical transition yet it may be a very effective and accurate jumper. So we are going for accuracy and balance above all else, and if we can bring the pony to anticipate a change of pace or direction so much the better. For when jumping-off against the clock, a pony that will anticipate a change of direction, and change his leading leg immediately on that change of direction, is the one that will save just that vital fraction of a second which can make the difference between first and second.

When the pony is unridden it is perfectly natural to him to make changes of pace with balance. Nobody tells him when to go from the trot to the canter. He decides everything for himself, preparing his body and point of balance in advance for the movement or pace he next intends. But, when ridden, he has to accept a rider's weight on his back, as well as obey commands of which he has no pre-knowledge. So the first thing we, as riders, must do is warn and prepare the pony for the action we wish to take. But the pony must not be hurried or excited by the actions of the rider when moving from either a slow pace to a fast one, or from a fast pace to a slow one.

The first step in preparing the pony for good, effective transitions is to practice control over the rhythm of his paces. One way of doing this is to count the beats of each gait as the pony's feet strike the ground. From your counting you will be able to judge the regularity of the pace. For example, in the walk, you should be counting something like, near-fore — 1, off-hind — 2, off-fore — 3, near-hind — 4; in the trot, near-fore/off-hind — 1, and off-fore/near-hind — 2; in the canter, both hindlegs — 1, off-fore — 2, and near-fore — 3. Once the pace is regulated then the pony will be attentive and concentrating, ready to obey the wishes of the rider. There is no point in asking a pony that is 'fresh' or 'above himself' through lack of work to execute a perfect transition. His mind will not be attentive. And as we train on the association of ideas principle, all exercises must be carried out under conditions that are going to lead to a successful result. Equally, it is no good asking a tired or unfit pony to answer the signals from the saddle with smoothness and accuracy. This little exercise of regulating the stride can be used to settle a pony and bring him to the right frame of mind for serious work. If you can think of a tune that fits each tempo, 4-beat, 2-beat and 3-beat, then hum it to yourself as you work and may help you to approach the training sessions with a clear and concentrated mind too!

Now during this work phase I have my riders sitting down in the saddle, especially in the trot. The rising trot is of no use to us here as in all the transitions the rider must be down and close to the pony.

Making the transition from a fast pace to a slower one is one of the most difficult transitions for the novice pony to execute properly. Many young riders, too, have their problems here. Often the rider makes the classic mistake of pulling on the reins to slow the pace, and losing contact with the pony's mouth when increasing the pace. If the rider pulls on the reins the pony's immediate reaction will be to pull back at the rider. So the transition becomes a battle of forces — who can pull the hardest. This presents an ugly, unbalanced picture which totally destroys the effectiveness of the whole of the training programme. So always remember that any pulling by the rider will only be answered by more pulling from the pony. This starts the downhill sequence to more severe bits and more complicated equipment.

So let us just talk through the transition from canter to trot: the rider applies the pressure of both legs to create more energy from the pony's hindlegs and then this extra energy is used as a 'brake' to come to the slower pace. As the rider applies his leg pressure he pushes down in the saddle with his seat bones, braces the small of his back, leans back slightly from the hip, closes his hands, firmly resisting the energy he is creating from behind through the reins. The pony gives to the resistance of the hands and changes down a 'gear' evenly but with power into a balanced active trot. Once in the trot the rider again regulates the rhythm of the pace ready for the next transition or change of direction.

For the transition from trot to canter, we need to bring in an extra element, which is the leading leg at the canter. The pony is said to be leading with a certain leg at the canter, according to the foreleg which is taking the longer stride. But we can add a further refinement in as much as the hindleg on the same side must also be moving at a slightly longer stride than its partner. So if the pony is leading with his near-fore then his near-hind will be taking a slightly longer stride than his off-hind and striking the ground fractionally in front of the off-hind. If the pony tends to lead with his near-fore but does not follow through with his near-hind then he is said to be cantering disunited. The word disunited speaks for itself — lack of balance — quite the opposite to the requirements we are looking for in the correctly produced jumping pony.

Practising the Leading Leg at the Canter The pony and rider (in the sitting position) trot to a corner of the manege and as they pass through that corner the rider 'asks' for the canter by pushing the pony up to his hands, squeezing with both legs but with the pressure

Raising the asking hand and placing the weight on the outside seat-bone to prepare and ask for a transition to the canter on the right lead.

increased and placed slightly further back from the leg opposite to the lead he requires from the pony. If, for example, the rider and pony are going around the arena anti-clockwise then the rider's stronger leg aid will be the right one, with the pony striking off with his near-fore leading (vice versa for the off-fore leading). The pony should strike off with the leading leg to the direction in which he is going. *But* we require a little more than this from our jumping pony for he must not only bend his complete body to the direction of his 'lead' but he must also be balanced and ready to face either a single fence or a line of fences. So as the rider asks for the leading leg, he must slightly raise the 'inside' hand to encourage the pony to bend to the direction and increase his body weight on his 'outside' seatbone to encourage the pony to keep his hindlegs engaged under him ready to give the power to the strides when approaching a fence. Now once this transition is perfected at corners, pony and rider are ready to take the next step working in circles. But if the leading leg is not attained at any time, or the pony shows a tendency to go disunited, then the pony must be brought back to the trot immediately and the entire sequence started again at the next corner.

As soon as smoothness and obedience has been achieved on straight lines and around corners in the arena, the pony must be taught to 'give' the individual parts of his body to the rider through the medium of aids. There are four main exercises that can be used to refine the jumping pony's education to the rider's aids. They are the turn on the forehand, the shoulder-in, the haunches-in, and the rein-back. Now the use of these movements for jumping training must not be confused with their uses for competition dressage; the aims of one are not the same as the other. In jumping training we are not looking for a pure classical style and execution, but we are looking for immediate and willing obedience.

Turn on the forehand exercise The pony is asked to move his hindquarters by crossing one hindleg over the other around his forehand. The pony should pivot on his foreleg or describe a small circle. In jumping training I am not too fussy about the pivot on the inside foreleg, a small circle will suffice, but I do want the pony to step across with the hindleg. So when turning to the right the off-

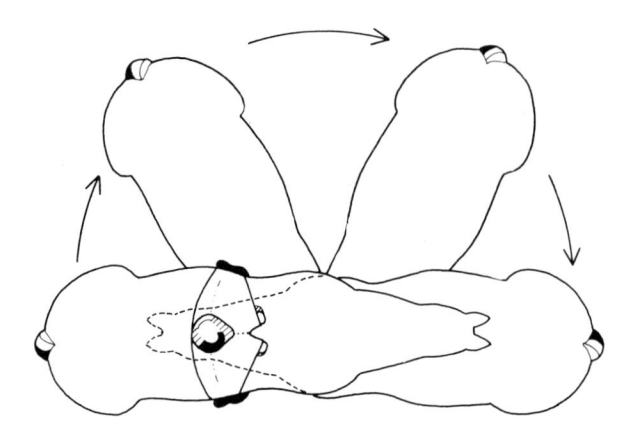

Fig. 9 The form the turn on the forehand should make.

fore will be describing a small circle. But it must not take a step backwards or forwards. The rider's right leg is drawn back behind the girth; a 'squeeze' is applied on the right rein by the right hand, but the pony's head must not be actually turned; the rider's left leg is held at the girth, to restrain the pony from stepping backwards, and to be ready to ask him to move forwards when the figure is completed. A schooling stick should be used when first starting this exercise to back-up the rider's 'asking' leg and to teach the pony to submit to the aid and move his haunches away.

I add to this gradually by first asking the pony to walk on briskly after the turn, then to trot on immediately, and finally to go straight away into the canter. My reason for doing this is that in show jumping we need total 'call' on the pony's hindquarters and power from any given position or angle. There is very little practical use in this turn in itself but it is a very efficient exercise for discipline, suppling and muscle building.

The Shoulder-in and the Haunches-in These are exercises designed to supple the pony's body, and continuous use of them will maintain suppleness. But, once again, we can add a bit more to that in relation to jumping training, for not only will and do these exercises work the pony in the gymnastic sense, but also a regular

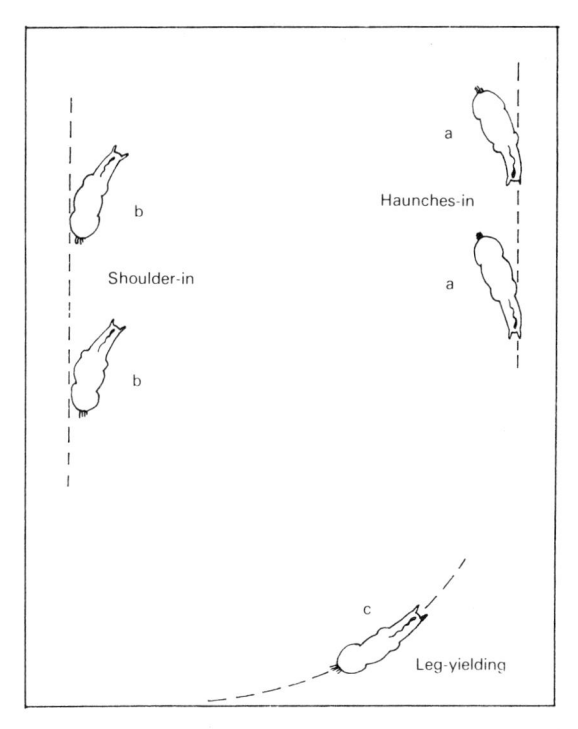

Fig. 10 Daily exercises in the training area encourage supple muscles, encourage the pony to yield to the asking leg aid and the active hand, and encourage calmness in the jumping pony.

programme of 'figure' work, before starting jumping schooling or in preparation for a contest, does have the added bonus of calming and concentrating the pony's mind. Mind you, they are not bad for riders either!

We start off quite simply by using the corners of the schooling arena to commence the exercise. As pony and rider come through the corner of the arena, the rider 'asks' with the left rein as if to continue with a complete circle to, say, the left. With the right rein the rider does not allow the pony to describe this circle. The rider's left leg is pressed at the girth, to encourage the pony to go forward on a line, and the right leg is placed slightly behind the girth to keep the hindlegs on the track. The hindquarters must stay on their original track while the pony moves forward with his right shoulder leading his left hip, and his left shoulder moving outside his left hip. This 'asks' the pony to bend his body around the pressure of the rider's left leg and to place his hocks well under him. Both actions produce overall suppleness and a powerful stride from the hindlegs. So, once again, by exercising the pony's ability to produce impulsion with the minimum effort and strain we will have power at our call in the jumping ring.

The exercise must be taken in slow, progressive stages, the rider asking for the movement for only very short sequences and, whether the rider gets the response he is asking for or not, the pony should be allowed to carry on and complete the normal circle. Eventually the pony will able to hold the shoulder-in attitude for the entire length of the exercise arena. The exercise, of course, should be worked up on both reins (directions).

The haunches-in is an exercise with exactly the same aims as the shoulder-in. But this time we are working on the control of the hindquarters. Again the figure should be started on a corner and working from a walk to a trot as soon as possible. This time the rider's left lower leg pushes the hindquarters (as it did in the turn on the forehand) away from the track of the forehand; the rider's left hand is closed (active) and the right hand is open (passive); the rider's right lower leg is kept at the girth to hold the forehand on the original track. (*Fig. 10*).

The Rein-Back is technically a forward movement and, to be of any value in jumping training, it must be treated as such. In other words, it is an active, positive figure in which the pony must submit to his bridle without resistance through his jaw, or back, and step backwards quite definitely and cleanly. It must not be a 'tugging' battle between pony and rider or a form of bad-tempered disciplining by the rider on the pony. (A sight which one sees all too often, even at international level, in the jumping arena.)

The pony should be standing squarely with a relaxed jaw to his bridle and, if possible, alongside one of the barriers of the schooling arena, or a wall, to encourage straightness in the movement. The rider 'asks' the pony to move forward in the normal way, that is to say squeezing the lower legs to the girth area and bracing the small of the back to lower the seat bones, but through his closed hands he does not allow the pony to move forward. The pony should give to the resistance of the rider's hands and step backwards with his forelegs and hindlegs. This must be started in very short sequences, one full stride back at first will be a very good result indeed. Now the rider must also ensure that the pony reins back straight on a single track, correcting any deviation with his leg aids in the same way as he controlled the pony's hindquarters in the turn on the forehand. The most important thing with the rein-back exercise used in this sense, preparation for jumping, is that it must be kept positive. The moment the movement is attained quickly, ask the pony to walk-on. Again I build this one up to rein-back/walk-on, rein-back/trot-on and rein-back/canter-on. This sharpens pony and rider mentally and works the pony's back, loin, forearm, shoulder and neck muscles. In other words, used in this way the rein-back can build up power.

The Half-halt This is one of the most important exercises in the groundwork for jumping and, in many cases, one the most neglected and misused. When we start working over fences and eventually competing in the show arena, we are going to need a pony that will 'come back' to us and 'go away' from us with smoothness, power and, above all, calmness. The half-halt is the absolute basis to this discipline; it encourages submission to the bridle, obedience to the rider's aids, balance and co-ordination in both pony and rider.

It is a simple exercise requiring no special facilities or even a great deal of room. As the pony trots down the long side of the schooling ring, or any other straight line such as along a paddock fence or hedgerow, the rider closes his hands resisting the forward movement of the pony, closes his lower legs to the girth, pushes down with his seat-bones. The pony will give to the closed hands of the rider and slow his rate of trot on a light contact. After a few paces the rider then asks the pony to trot on again by gradually opening his fingers, increasing his leg and seat aids. That is all there is to it really, but it is all the little nuances and refinements which the exercise will show up and encourage that is its value in jumping

The half-halt exercise. In the second picture we can see the rider asking for the slower pace. In the third picture we can see the pony really lengthen his stride. Study particularly that near hindleg stride.

54

training. For example, if the pony stiffens his jaw and resists the closed hands of the rider, or shows signs of getting excited, then that pony is not ready yet for serious groundwork and should be taken back to elementary schooling to be re-mouthed either by a lightweight adult or a very experienced young rider. Equally, the pony may shows signs of being reluctant to move forward freely away from the rider's leg and seat aids. Again this is of no use to us for jumping because the jumping pony *must* move forward well, with complete willingness. The pony will never attack fences if he is slow or reluctant to yield to the leg aid. It would be back to the drawing board once more if this trait showed itself. So the little half-halt exercise executed at the trot and canter, going long strides, short strides, long strides, can tell us all we want to know about pony and rider and from this information the decision can be taken on just how near they are to being ready for jumping schooling.

Circle work and changes of direction I never start serious circle work until I am absolutely happy with the pony through his transitions, obedience to aids and bridle, and his collection because, on a modern show jumping course, apart from the fences to be jumped, the 'track', which is the path pony and rider are going to take around the course, will often contain two, even three, changes of rein, and on the jump-off course there will nearly always be a complete 'turn-back' to a fence. So balanced, smooth turns are as much part of success in the show ring as jumping the fences cleanly. Therefore, improving pony and rider's technique at circles and changes of direction is as important as the technique of jumping.

The golden rule of riding a circle is to keep the pony straight! That sounds a bit strange doesn't it? But it is not as silly as it sounds, for in riding we say a pony is straight when the track of the hindlegs follows directly behind the track of the forelegs. So in circle work the pony must move on a single track. The hindquarters must not swing out and the shoulder must not lean in. A good example of the practical application of these principles is the technique of riding at an indoor show. The corners of the indoor arena must be used to maximum advantage by the competitior because indoors the fences come more quickly and often the pony will have to be asked to

William giving us a perfect demonstration of bending, or flexing, to his circle while staying on a single track and maintaining the power of his stride.

come off a corner and go down a line of fences. The corner itself represents a quarter of a circle and the deeper the pony and rider go into that corner the better they will meet the fences to come. But if a pony will not bend into the corner, or comes out of it leading with his shoulder, then his hindquarters will literally be left behind. The total results are the loss of power and the loss of rhythm in the stride.

The two most important principles governing changes of direction and circle work are: (a) The pony must bend his complete body to the curve of the circle or the change of rein. Yet the bend of the pony's neck must not be greater than the bend of his body, (b) The pony must move on a single track. We attain these two principles by the independent use of our hand, seat and leg aids. When changing direction to, say, the left, the left hand is the asking hand but the right hand supports it by keeping contact with the pony's mouth and so not allowing the head position to change from the direction in which pony and rider are travelling. The rider's inside leg stays at the girth to encourage the pony to bend his body from the middle and the rider's asking hand is slightly raised to flex the pony to the direction. The rider's outside leg works behind the girth controlling the hindquarters, and his body weight is carried on his outside seat-bone.

For the jumper we not only require balanced, smooth changes of direction, we also need a change of the leading leg with each change of rein. For this we use, at first, a figure of eight and then two circles next to each other. On the figure of eight, let us say the pony is cantering on his right lead, then, as he comes round to go down the diagonal of the eight, the rider brings him back to the trot. As he begins the next turn, the rider asks him to canter again but this time on his left lead. Now the secret at this stage is repitition, if the pony gets the wrong lead at any time the rider must bring him back to the trot and start all over again. In other words, a sort of self-illustration to the pony that he will only be allowed to canter away quietly when he is on the correct lead. Eventually the rider will begin to feel the pony anticipate the change of lead and that is the reaction we want from a jumper. Now the work on two circles can begin.

This time the pony is cantered, say, on a right-hand circle leading with his off-fore, then when the rider feels the pony is settled and balanced he brings the pony back to a trot, quickly changes to a left-handed circle and asks for the near-fore to lead. The distance of the trot is progessively shortened and the rider must shift his weight in the saddle according to the direction. For example, on a right circle the rider's weight is on his left seat-bone and on a left circle on his right seat-bone. Eventually the pony will once more begin to anticipate the change of lead with the change of direction, and the rider will find the pony making the change himself almost instantaneously with the change of direction. I find this 'teach-yourself' system is the best with ponies, rather than a more technical approach, such as attempting the flying change, which usually results in the pony changing his lead in front but not behind. If the pony does not anticipate, in other words teach himself, then it is better to use the short trot and change than to attempt more complicated techniques. Even in the competition arena I would still stick to simple methods where there is little or no chance of anything going wrong.

5 The Lunge-Rein and Practice Fences

Now that we have completed our groundwork and brought the pony up to an educated, responsive and obedient ride we can begin the gymnastic training for the real meat of the training programme — jumping.

This is where *cavalletti* work begins — the wall-bars of jumping training, and here we have two aims, (a) Efficient control over the length of the pony's strides, and (b) Effective muscle building and suppling of the pony's joints. I do not use real cavalletti for this work, instead I use coloured poles on the ground and/or slightly raised ones. After all, it is coloured rails the pony is going to jump in the ring, so the sooner these are used and he gets confident working over them the better.

We start our ponies off by being led on a headcollar over just one single pole, and then over two, and finally over three. These poles are just laid flat on the ground. All we are aiming to do here is to give the pony confidence over the poles and let him see what we are

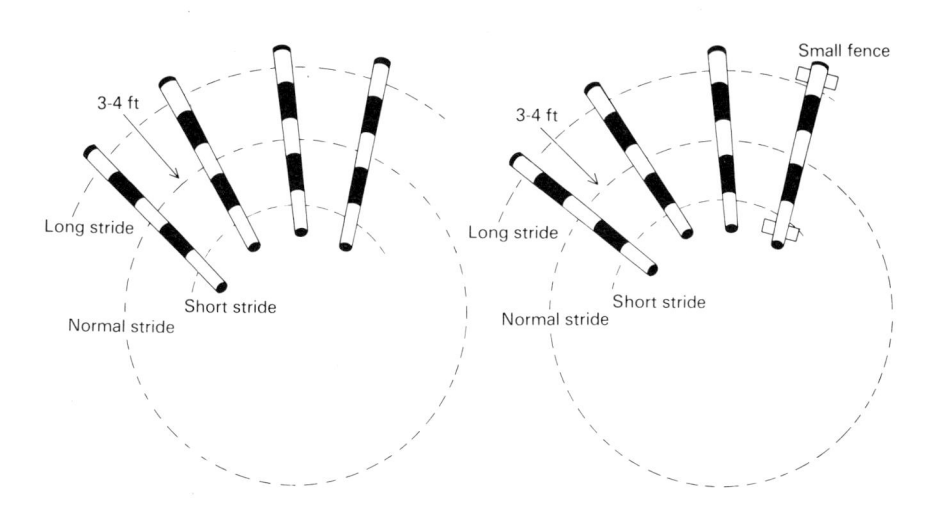

Fig. 11 Layout of rails on the ground for lungeing exercises.
Fig. 12 Layout of rails on the ground with a small fence for lungeing exercises.

Leading over the rail on the ground before starting the exercise seriously.

First introduction after leading — lungeing with no side-reins.

going to be asking him to do. Then we place the poles in a gentle curve set about 45 to 60 cm (1 ft 6 in to 2 ft) apart at the inner area of the curve and 1 m to 1.2 m (3 ft 6 in to 4 ft) apart at the outer area of the curve. These distances can be but a guide as the stride of each varies and the stride of an untrained pony is quite different to that of the trained pony. But by trial and error the suitable distance for each pony can soon be found. As the pony walks down over the poles his strides should be even. If they are not, then the distances must be re-set until the even stride is attained.

On the lunge we use a roller and elastic side-reins. These simulate control to the pony so that he relates the trotting over the poles to being under complete control. This is the situation we are going to put him in when we start 'real' jumping. The side-reins have the added effect of making the pony elevate his strides while forcing him to work his neck, back, shoulders and loins. But side-reins should not be used on a pony that is uneducated in his mouth, or shows resistance to his bridle, and never with any complicated form of bit, such as a curb bit.

The pony is lunged over the three rails on the ground in both directions. Once he has begun to regulate his stride and flex his joints so that he trots over them evenly with an elevated gait, we can then add an extra refinement to the exercise. By using the inner area of the curve we can make the pony shorten his stride and by using the outer area of the curve we can make him lengthen his stride.

Having taught the pony to regulate his stride while under simulated control, we can now move on to encouraging him to adapt this technique to actually jumping a small obstacle. This can be done on the circle, but I prefer to stay with the simplest possible situation by going back to a straight line. What we do this time is to lay out two trotting poles on the ground set at a suitable distance to allow *one step* (not a stride) in between each pole. This normally would be about 75 to 90 cm (2 ft 6 in to 3 ft), but the last pole is set back from the small jump by at least one full stride and, again, this would be somewhere around 1.8 to 2.4 m (6 ft to 8 ft), depending on the stride of the pony.

We try to make the small fence look as much like a real show

In the first picture Fiddler is working on the short stride distance, in the second on the normal stride distance, and in the third on the long stride distance. Notice how the short side-reins encourage the pony to elevate his action and regulate his strides.

Try to make the small fence look like a show fence.

jumping fence as possible by dressing it with trees, flowers or anything else colourful and different that we can find. So the pony now is beginning to work seriously to show fences. The side-reins are still kept fairly short but not as short as they were over the trotting poles. In other words we start to let the pony begin to feel some freedom of his head and neck as he would under saddle. Then we take the trotting poles away progressively as we see him graduate to a regulated even stride and absolute accuracy over the fence. Once this has been attained, we add a second fence set at a distance to allow one full stride from landing over the first to taking-off for the second fence. Now we can start bringing in variety by making the first fence a small vertical and the second fence a small spread. These preliminary fences should start at about 60 cm (2 ft) in height, with the spread set as a near-parallel of about 60 cm (2 ft) and, say 68 cm (2 ft 3 in) in height, and width again of about 60 cm

(2 ft). As the pony improves his technique the fences can be raised and widened gradually to a maximum of about 90 cm. But at this stage we are not looking for a big jump from the pony, we are looking for a good technique, clean jumping and suspension in the air over the fence. So heights are not really all that important yet. As this phase is perfected, we add a third fence, again set to allow one full stride from landing to point of take-off.

If the groundwork and preparatory work has been done correctly, with patience and sensitivity, there should be no problems, but if there are then take the pony back to the previous exercise and work up to the difficult area again. Don't fall into the trap of forcing the pony to jump at this stage, we want him to teach himself so force will defeat this object. If the pony shows a tendency to get excited about his jumping and rushes his fences then the more trotting poles you place in front of the fence the more he will be discouraged from rushing and he will eventually jump his fences calmly.

The next stage is to work under saddle and for this we go back a few paces to the trotting poles on the ground. The trotting poles are laid out on the two sides of the schooling arena so that we have two grids. On one side three poles are laid out 'short' with distances between them of some 76 to 90 cm (2 ft 6 in to 3 ft), on the other side they are set out 'long' that is with distances of 90 cm to 1 m 67 cm (3 ft to 3 ft 6 in).

The training programme is carried out at the sitting trot only and the direction, left-handed or right-handed, is changed about every 8 to 10 minutes. The rider's job is to guide the pony down the middle of the grids regulating the pace to slow, short strides for the 'short' grid and longer, more powerful strides for the 'long' grid. So the rider must use all his aids, hands, legs and seat-bones, to keep impulsion and regularity in the pony's gait. If the pony shows any signs of resisting the bridle, by stiffening the jaw or pulling at the rider, then take him back to working on the lunge in the side-reins. Before long the pony will soon start flexing his joints and suspending his steps to negotiate each grid and the rider will feel the pace change to an active rocking rhythm down the grids. Once this stage has been reached, the pony is well on the way to becoming a show jumper having learned to control each step with accuracy and power.

The trotting poles have been raised. Just look how William is flexing those joints and regulating his stride!

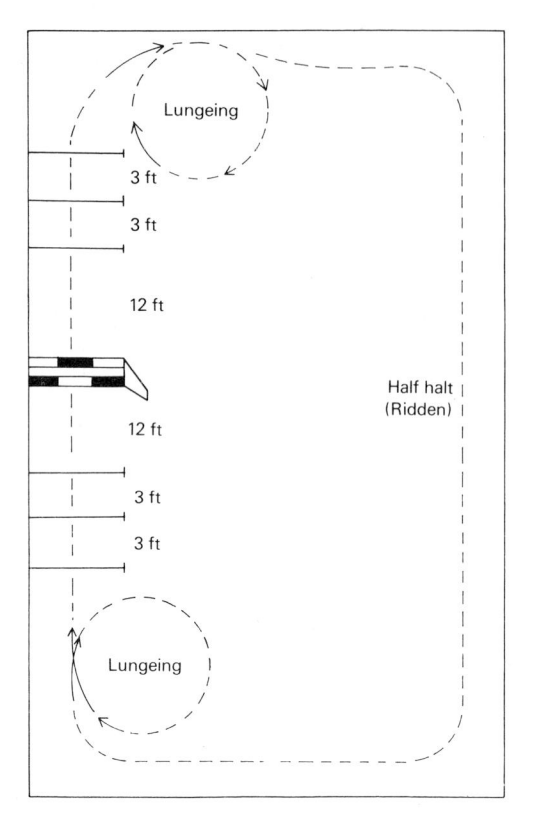

Fig. 13 Layout of trotting poles with a spread fence. The distances can be played with and fences added as the trotting poles are taken away.

A long schooling stick should be used throughout this phase — not to beat the pony with but to back up the rider's leg and seat aids. Young children up to about 12-years-old do not have a great deal of strength in their leg and seat aids, so a small flick with the schooling stick will help to make the pony 'listen' to their aids. I would rather see a young rider working with the schooling stick under supervision than see them kicking and thumping with their heels like some Thelwell cartoon character. There is more than enough for the rider to be doing in jumping without the added complication of swinging his, or her, legs all over the place. And the pony, too, must find this flapping around an aggravating handicap.

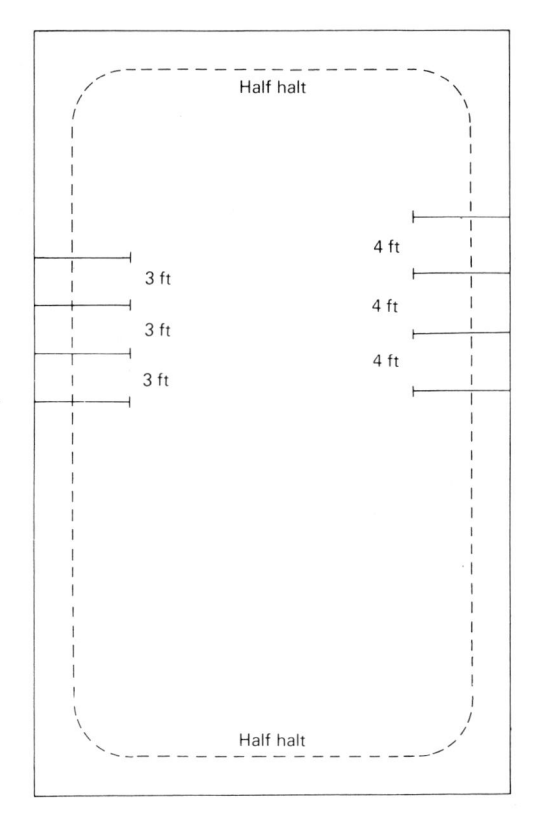

Fig. 14 Layout of trotting poles for work under saddle.

As soon as the pony starts 'bouncing' cleanly down the grids, the trotting poles can be raised slightly to flex his joints more and to ask for extra accuracy from him. We do this by simply resting the ends of the poles on the barrier of the schooling ring. But any system, such as placing bricks under each end of the poles, will do the job just as well. Now this time we vary the programme by changing from just simply trotting around the arena to making a circle from the centre of the arena to the grids: sometimes a small circle giving a short, angled approach to each grid, and sometimes a large circle, giving a long, angled approach to each grid. Again we keep up the exercise each day until the pony is suspending his steps and bouncing down the grids evenly.

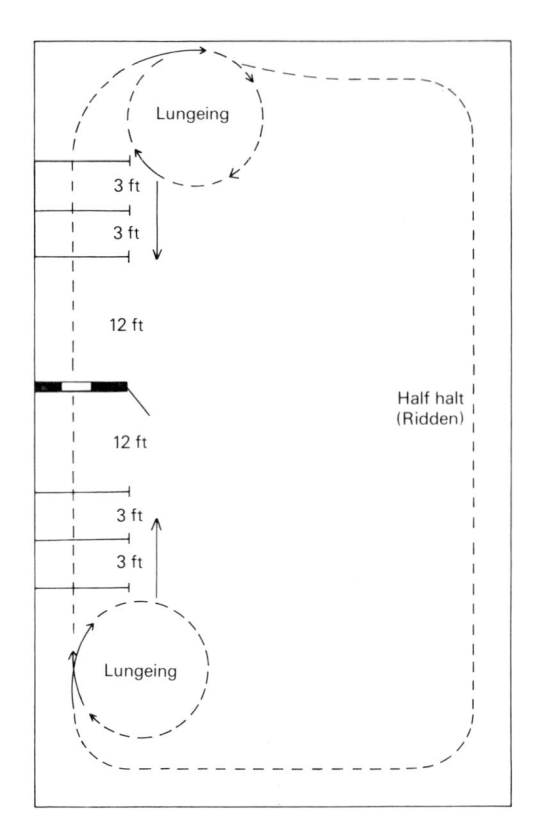

Fig. 15 Layout of trotting poles with a vertical fence, for work on the lunge or under saddle. (Note that the distances are based on a pony with an 8—9 ft stride.)

A good jumping technique is based upon sound knowledge of rhythm and timing, and that goes for the pony and the rider. So now that we have brought rhythm and timing into the pony's vocabulary, as it were, we can begin to work on the rider as well. Until now the rider has done nothing much more than he or she would have done on any advanced or intermediate equitation course, but now that the jumping of obstacles, our final phase, has been reached the rider, too, must work on technique and timing.

We stay with the two grids of poles on the ground but now add to them a small fence, as we did in the work on the lunge. On one side where we have the 'short' grid we will place a small vertical and on the other where we have the 'long' grid we will place a small spread, a near-parallel as before. (Although there are a tremendous variety of fences in show jumping they basically come down to the vertical and the spread so this is all we will need at this stage).

Conditions are now getting nearer to actual jumping. Pony and rider know where the poles are and where the small fences are and the pony has shown the rider the pace, stride and activity he needs to negotiate both grids. So the pony now must be encouraged to jump from that pace with the power of his hindquarters before the rider can begin to bring accuracy into his technique to compliment that of the pony. This phase I call *free-style schooling*, for the want of a better term, because that is precisely what we are going to do — allow the pony as much freedom as possible to put himself right for each fence. Once more this programme will be carried out at the sitting trot.

For the small upright on the 'short' grid the rider will feel the pony looking for his point of take-off and that point will be closer to the fence than for the little spread to come. Further, the rider will notice that the pony lowers his head slightly and extends his neck as he sees that point of take-off. The rider should then 'ride' the trotting poles but on passing over the last one should give the pony complete freedom from the bridle, riding only with leg and seat aids. As soon as the pony has landed and recovered the rider brings him under complete control again ready for the 'long' grid. At the 'long' grid the rider again 'rides' the trotting poles but on passing over the last pole gives the pony complete freedom of the bridle, though this time applying his leg and seat aids much more strongly than for the vertical, thereby encouraging the pony to go for height and length in the air. A few days of this programme and the pony will start anticipating what type of jump he will need purely by relating it to the pressure of the rider's aids, i.e. more pressure for length and height, and a steady pressure for height only. So when pony and rider eventually arrive at the competition arena the pony will respond immediately to the rider's technique.

Now as the pony is being left to teach himself, or rather to help himself to his fences, the rider will be learning the stride the pony needs to negotiate each fence cleanly by concentrating on the feel

Now there is only one rail on the ground and you can see William measuring his fence.

The pony has met his fence right and jumped it correctly. Addy has given him the chance to help himself.

No rails on the ground. Addy has seen her stride too late but she has given William the freedom to get himself out of trouble.

and rhythm. There will be occasions when the pony will make corrections to his balance and movement. For instance, the pony may just slightly check his stride on approaching a ground pole, or slightly rush at the first pole of the grid. On another occasion the pony may fractionally — mistime his stride over the last trotting poles and then put in a short stride before taking off at the fence. Or he may take too long a stride and find himself too close to the fence, forcing himself to strain his body to get into the air, or to knock a rail off the fence. The rider will see and feel all these conditions and begin to anticipate them. Once this stage is reached the rider has started to 'see a stride' at a fence; the magical, but not mythical, ingredient vital to every jumping rider's technique. So the rider is now asked to start riding all the way to the fences. He now knows where the pony's point of take-off should be and how to regulate the stride and control the power of that stride. The whole programme can now be worked at the canter with the fences going up one hole at a time.

With ponies like William and Fiddler I like to keep them at this phase until they are jumping at least a vertical of 90 cm to 1 m (3 ft to 3 ft 3 in) and a spread of at least 90 cm (3 ft), and until my daughter Addie can convince me that she is really seeing a stride at each grid. Then we start to take the trotting poles away one at a time and work on circles with long, angled approaches and short, angled approaches.

Solving the Problems

So our jumper is now on his way, but what about the problems? Well, there will be problems. Wouldn't it be nice if one could say this, this...and that...and this...with no horrible little 'but' at the end. *But* (there it is!) problems are as much part of the show jumping game as they are of any other sport. So let us take a look at some of the more common problems which can arise, in the hope

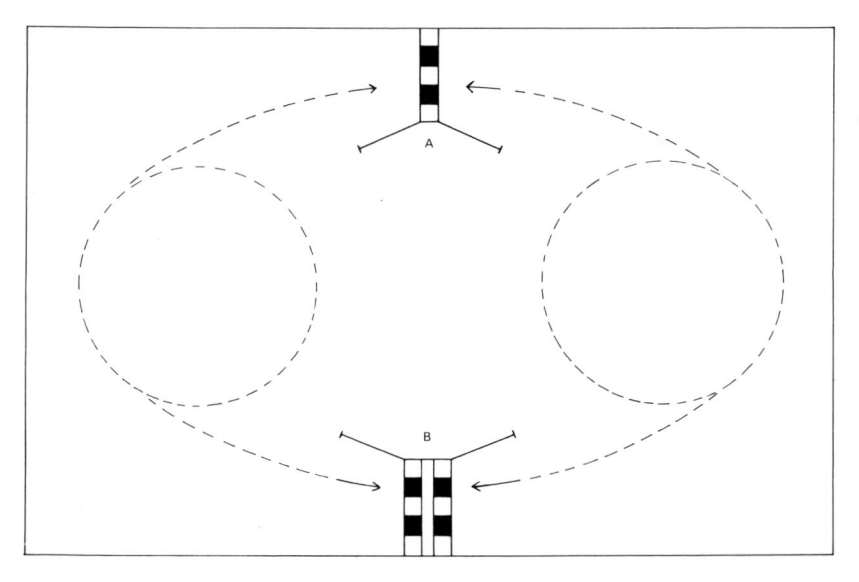

Fig. 16 Working on circles with practice fences: a) a vertical, and b) a spread.

Pony and rider meeting the fence right on a short approach. Notice, by the way, how even a simple X-rail fence can be made to look imposing.

that this will help you to eradicate them at the earliest possible stage, rather than at the practice stage before going into the show arena. Which, by the way, is often too late.

The pony rushing his fences The pony that does this or gets excited about jumping schooling, is usually telling us he is not confident of his jumping ability. The best method to encourage him to be calmer about his jumping is to keep the trotting poles in front of his schooling fences until he does go in and jump calmly. If he still continues to rush then put him back on the lunge with the elastic side-reins fitted and place two poles on the ground on the landing side. In other words, you must give him much more to think about, to keep his mind off worrying about the obstacle itself, and make the fences low and easy.

Pony refusing at his fences This is a delicate question — what to do about the pony that puts in a stop. For some he is the worst kind. But is he? I would rather have the intelligent pony that will 'stop' at a fence, in effect saying, 'Oh, no! This one's a bit too big for me!' or 'Oops, I've met this one wrong, nothing doing!' and then come round a second time, get it right and jump it cleanly than the not so intelligent pony, but perhaps too brave, who will carry on regardless, crash through the fence and possibly injure himself and his rider. True enough, in a competition the winners are the pony and rider that will meet a problem at a fence, live with it, pull themselves together, cock their ears, stick out their little jaws, and go for the next one as if nothing had happened. But at that level we are concerned with the experienced and confident competitors. At the moment we are thinking about the inexperienced and not so confident. True bravery can only come from confidence and skill, and without those two factors bravery can often be fool-hardy.

So, if the pony stops at a fence, look for the reasons. Was his approach correct? Did the rider present the pony to the fence incorrectly? Is the fence too big for the pony at this stage? Is the rider nervous of jumping? Once these factors have been analysed, lower the fence and come round to it again bringing it back progressively to its original dimensions. But if the pony is an habitual stopper, even with a light adult on board, then the horrible truth

The pony has jumped the first element of a double well enough, but the pony looks stiff and the rider is giving it no freedom to use its body. The pony takes a stride, tries for the second element...but....oops!...it can't make it!

must be faced, he is not going to make a show jumper. In that situation find something else for him to do because often a pony that cannot adapt to show fences will go and jump cross-country fences at the faster pace with absolute willingness and success.

The Pony running-out at his fences Once again, this is a sign of lack of confidence, or an intense dislike of jumping. (Although it can often be just plain cheekiness when a pony feels he can take charge of his young rider). Two rails placed either side of each fence resting on the wings will usually solve this problem, or a few schooling sessions with a lightweight adult in the saddle. But if these fail then once more one must face the fact that that particular pony will not make a show jumper. If a pony really dislikes jumping it is no use forcing him. The pony will become frightened and a dangerous ride for a child. Dangerous rides do not win red ribbons. Many of the problems met in jumping training are often caused by ourselves through lack of thought and care. So let us take a look at some of the more common areas where we can cause problems for ourselves.

Some Causes of Problems

Bad fitting tack and incorrect bitting Often a rider or trainer will find a pony jumps willingly enough but is inclined to be careless. Often the reason for this is quite simple and can be found in bad-fitting tack. So check that the saddle fits the pony well, see if there is any movement by the saddle when the pony is jumping, get some expert advice on its size and weight and check that the girth is not pinching him. We use thin show-girths most of the time, for example, because we find these give the pony's 'working parts', so to speak, the maximum freedom to operate efficiently. Make a very careful check of the bridle, see it fits properly and is not pinching the pony somewhere, such as around the ears and, particularly, the mouthpiece. See that it is the right size for the pony, especially around the lips.

That brings us on to the very delicate and complicated question of what type of bit to use. This is a difficult one to advise on and we would require a book on its own to discuss it properly. We use mainly snaffle bits with a dropped noseband, and for schooling and training only we add the draw-reins and side-reins. We do not use martingales, and because we buy all our ponies very young to 'make' ourselves we know they have no mouth problems and are not likely to develop any. But often a small problem in jumping can be solved by using a different bit, and that bit may not be harsh or cruel. I think international show jumping rider Harvey Smith, a real expert on bits and bitting, sums it all up when he says, '... there's a bit for every horse somewhere. What suits one doesn't suit another. Some bits and combinations of bits may look harsh, but some horses relax in them... Any real horseman knows that the moment you abuse a horse in the mouth you can put him in the field. Because if you have no mouth then you have no horse.'

David Broome, one of the most natural horsemen in the international arena anywhere in the world today. Just look at the simple equipment he has on his old favourite Queensway Sportsman.

So get expert advice on bitting if you think you have bridle problems.

Incorrect, or negative, presentation by the rider This is, perhaps, the most common cause of careless jumping in the show ring: poor presentation of the pony to his fences by the rider. It is a simple problem to try to put right. The rider should be able to feel that his pony is not 'meeting' his fences right, if he can't, then he is not ready to compete seriously. The trainer also should be able to see that pony and rider are not meeting their fences well, or that the rider is not attacking his fences with a positive technique. So this problem can be solved by putting in much more extra homework on the presentation until it is right. But if the rider continues to be weak in this area then his coach must take him back to the grids to do 'rhythm' work again and again until he really understands the importance of the pony's jumping technique in terms of stride, distance, activity and balance. To sum up this subject we can turn to Mr Fred Broome, senior, who says, 'Presentation has got to be absolutely 100%, or perhaps it is fairer to say 98% correct, otherwise you unbalance your horse...and that costs you a rail! It's as simple as that really.'

So study carefully what you are doing and how you are doing it. Over-riding a pony at a fence can cause just as many problems as under-riding; the art of a good effective jumping technique is a balance between the two.

Lack of training This can be overcome by returning to schooling on the flat. The pony, or horse, should not be put into a serious jumping training programme until he is going perfectly, that is to say working willingly to the rider's aids, on the flat. Equally, the rider should not start jumping training until he or she has an independent seat and is fully conversant with the techniques of riding on the flat.

Faulty training Bad memories of another rider or trainer, or a bad fall, will result in a loss of confidence. Patience, understanding and long, quiet hours of work are the only solution to these problems.

Lack of condition, or poor health A cause often overlooked because a pony can often look healthy yet have something bothering him. So have the pony checked for soreness (especially of shins), for lameness, for a sore back or a pulled muscle in the back, for ill-fitting shoes, etc. Get his teeth looked at. See that he is eating all his food. If there is any obvious lack of condition, such as sudden loss of flesh, or signs of worms, then rest the pony and consult your veterinarian.

6 Practice Makes Perfect

All that is needed now is practice and polishing of techniques before the moment of truth — the first public outing. Practice, they say, makes perfect, and no matter how threadbare that may sound it is no less than the only way to success. Some may and can take short-cuts to the top but they have a habit of slipping down to the 'second division' by the shortest of all routes. The really top-notch performer comes from the practical and real school of 'rehearse, rehearse and rehearse again'. This is particularly true of competitive show jumping whether it be in Great Britain, France, Australia or the United States of America. It is also true in Russia, East Germany, Poland and Hungary. To be successful in show jumping today, whether junior or senior, your horse or pony must be totally responsive and deadly accurate; your riding must be completely effective all the way from the warming-up ring to crossing the finishing line.

But it is often in this practice phase that many trainers and novice riders are tempted to disregard the graduated training programme by trying to take on more than they have the confidence to tackle. Any impetuosity at this stage can destroy weeks of careful training. So hasten slowly. Take one step at a time and do not move on to the next stage until you feel absolutely confident that you know what you are doing and that your pony knows what he is doing. If you have set a timetable for the training programme and the pony falls behind, then more often than not it is the schedule and not the pony that is in need of revamping.

For this finishing-off stage we move from the grids and single fences to the jumping lane, or chute, and a full practice course.

The jumping lane encourages suppleness and quick relexes in both the pony and the rider (*Fig. 4*). Once the pony has entered the chute the rider can concentrate and relax, simply riding forward, thinking about presentation to each fence and maintaining good rhythm as the fences come along in a regulated sequence. Once the pony can come down the chute at a steady regulated canter 'popping' over low oxers, double 'X' bars and a small gate calmly

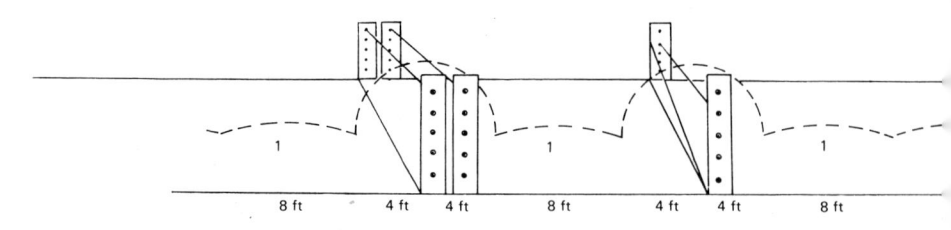

Fig. 17 Sample layout for exercise on even strides in a straight line: one non-jumping stride in each double, and five strides to the second double. (Based on a pony with an 8 ft stride — about 13 hh.)

and cleanly, then he is ready to make the transition to a laid-out course of show fences.

Many ponies find the transition from jumping straight lines of fences to a laid-out course with changes of direction in a wide open space an invitation to quicken their pace or to get excited about their jumping. So to alleviate this temptation the practice course should first be set very low, and the pony trotted over the first fence, and then asked to canter over the second. But if he shows signs of quickening too much, then trot over the first two fences and canter to the third and so on. It may be that you will have to trot to each fence for a couple days to keep the pony calm and accurate.

At this stage we like to present our ponies to the first fence then on landing circle, say, to the right, then come round and jump the second fence, circle to the left and so on. I find this system encourages the pony (and rider) to collect himself quickly on landing and gives the rider a better chance of making a good presentation to each fence. We even use this circling/jump/circling exercise in double combinations and treble combinations. If the pony has been brought through his groundwork and obedience training correctly, this circling exercise will not tempt or teach him to run-out or duck-out at his fences. On the contrary, it should make the pony more responsive and supple. We continue with this work for at least a week, gradually decreasing the circumference of the circles to encourage the pony to bend cleanly and give his mouth to the bridle after and before each fence. After some two weeks of this work your pony should be able to a negotiate a small course of show fences smoothly, rhythmically and, most of the time, cleanly.

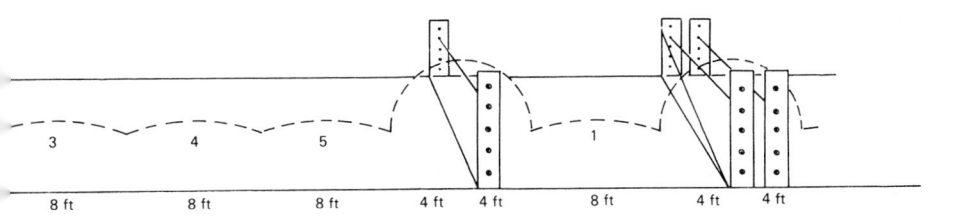

So we can now start bringing it all together, first, by summing up the aims and objects of working over practice fences:

1. The main object of the exercise is to improve technique and performances — so this must be seen to be done. If it is not, then somebody is not really working, or thinking, and it is back to the drawing board!

2. The course should be as varied as possible with the fences 'dressed' with any interesting material you can lay your hands on like flower boxes, small trees, base boards or cut birch.

3. The course should be determined beforehand and the rider made to walk the course so that he or she can get into the habit of thinking and talking through the approaches and distances.

4. The dimensions of the fences should at first be very, very easy, progressing to heights of 76 cm to 1.2 m (2 ft 6 in to 3 ft 6 in) and spreads of 90 cm to 1.2 m (3 ft to 3 ft 6 in).

5. If there are any problems, then take the pony back to the jumping chute to calm him and regain his confidence.

6. Variety is the spice of life, so change the layout of the course from time to time.

7. Always finish a schooling session on a good note. If things have gone well and the pony has jumped a good practice round, then finish on that. If things have not gone too well, then lower the fences and trot the pony over two or three fences and finish on that.

To maintain continuity, always have someone with you during practice sessions. Not necessarily a professional coach, but a person that is involved who can spot faults and help you and the pony to better your performance. That same person can re-build fences or replace fallen poles, saving you a great deal of time and frustration.

Always be in search of knowledge and advice, seek out and listen to constructive comments on your pony's and your own performance from other experienced horse people. Ask them to come down to watch you on a practice session one morning. If you can, think about taking some private lessons at this stage or joining a show jumping clinic. Most national federations, riding clubs and training centres organize teach-ins or clinics, often under very well-known trainers. Top international riders, amateur and professional, profit from the observant attention of coaches as a part of the game, so why not you and your jumping pony?

Now that the pony is jumping a simple but not all that small course of show fences, the time has come for the final stages of the training programme. We can test the pony with distances and approaches, as the course designer will do when pony and rider get into real competition. We do this by setting an exercise using three fences and by playing with the double and treble combinations.

The three-fence exercise

This is a sort of 'three-finger' exercise for jumping riding. We set three individual fences, a vertical, a parallel and an oxer, to form a triangle. (*Fig. 18*). This layout gives pony and rider a design on which they can practise angled approaches, distances and optional approaches. By now we should know accurately the stride of our novice jumping pony so we can set the triangle to give, say, a four to five stride even distance on the angle between fence one and/or fence two and three.

First, the pony and rider settle into a nice active and rhythmic canter on a circle in front of fence one. (Just off-centre of fence one in fact). Then when the rider feels the pony is supple and 'listening' to him he brings the pony in to jump fence one, on landing he canters on down the arena and turns on his right rein to jump fence two, but this time on landing he comes round on his right rein and goes for fence three. From fence three pony and rider turn on the

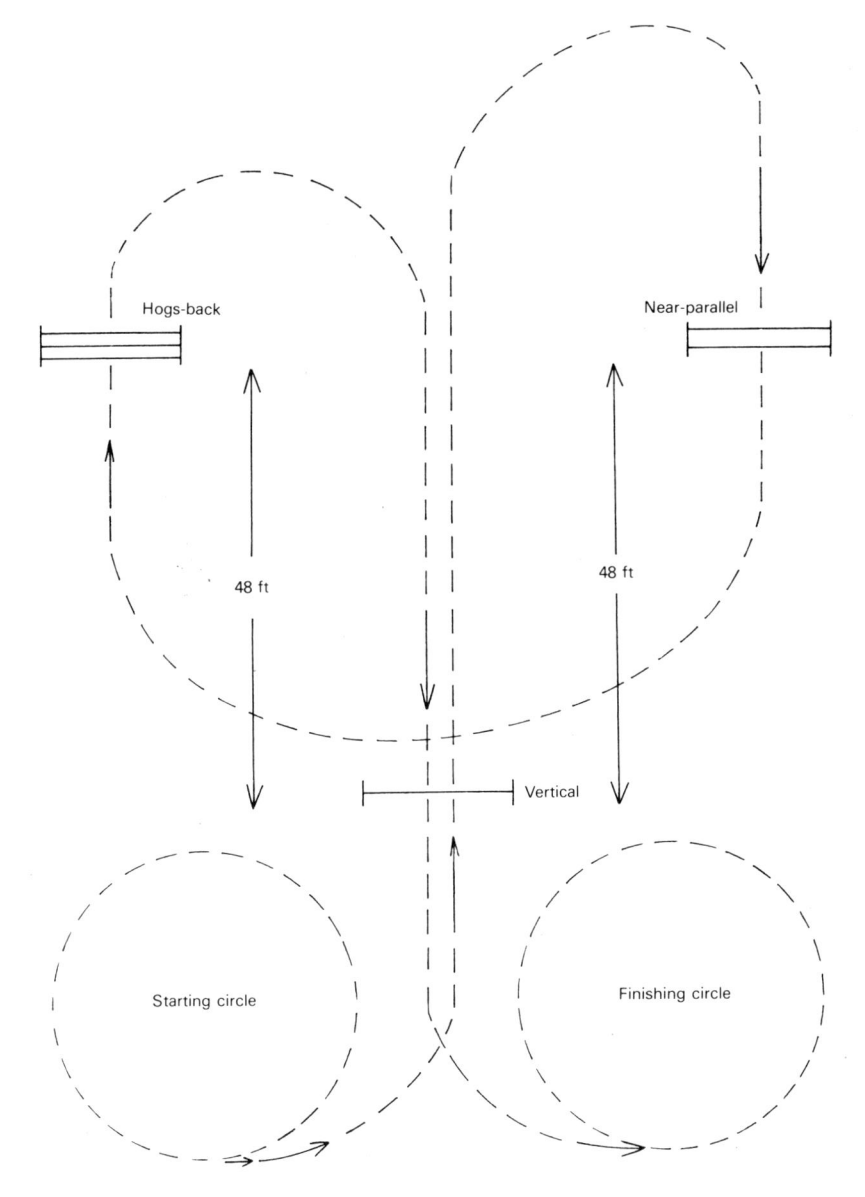

Fig. 18 A three-fence exercise showing one track that can be taken. Of course, there can be, and should be, several variations. Once more, the distances will depend on the length of the pony's stride.

right rein to jump fence one again and return to the circle at the canter. Now this can be varied between working on the left rein and working on the right rein.

Following this exercise we can start to make it more complicated, still only working with three fences. This time pony and rider jump fence one at an angle (still approaching from a circle) then they must regulate their stride, by counting 1, 2, 3, 4 and 5, for example, and go for fence two on the angle. From fence two pony and rider make a turn-back to jump fence one the other way, and on the other angle prepare themselves for turn-back to fence three. The variations that can be achieved on this simple triangle design are almost endless, working on angled approaches, angled jumps and judging even distances.

Double and treble distances

For this exercise a course designer sets his distances between each element to suit the average stride but he can also use this criterion to test his competitors on the flat. Say, for example, he allows 2.4 m (8 ft) as being the average stride for a 12.2 hh to 13 hh pony then by playing with the distances between his elements in double or treble combinations he can make that a 'long' 2.4 m (8 ft), by making it, say, 2.5 m (8 ft 3 in), or a 'short' 2.4 m (8 ft), by making it 2.3 m (7ft 9 in). By doing this he is giving the rider the option of getting in one even long stride or one even short stride, as he rides through the combination (*Fig. 19*). So we must do the same at home. Let us say we have been allowing one normal stride in the double combinations and in the treble combination one normal stride and two normal strides. Let us further assume that we have calculated the stride of our jumping pony is about 2.4 m (8 ft). So in the double combination we have been leaving enough room between the elements to give an even 2.4 m (8 ft) non-jumping stride. As we have been watching the pony through his whole training programme we know almost exactly where he lands over the first element, and where he takes off for the second, so it is easy to allow the 2.4 m (8 ft) non-jumping stride in the middle. The same goes for our practice treble combinations. So we can now give pony and rider experience of regulating their stride in the combinations.

Fig. 19 Setting distance problems in double combinations. (From right to left)

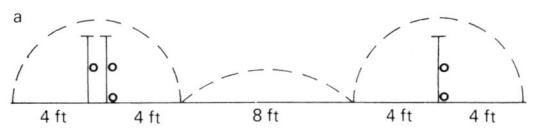

a

4 ft   4 ft   8 ft   4 ft   4 ft

Set at one even non-jumping stride.

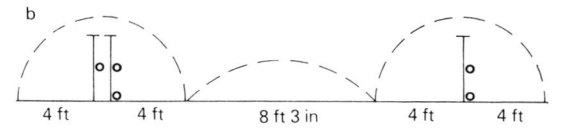

b

4 ft   4 ft   8 ft 3 in   4 ft   4 ft

Set at one long non-jumping stride.

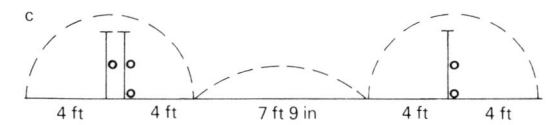

c

4 ft   4 ft   7 ft 9 in   4 ft   4 ft

Set at one short non-jumping stride.
(Based on a pony with an 8 ft stride — about 13 hh.)

Fig. 20 Setting distance problems in treble combinations. (From right to left)

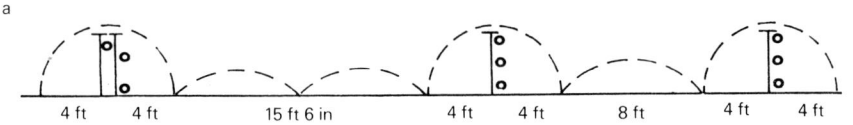

a

4 ft   4 ft   15 ft 6 in   4 ft   4 ft   8 ft   4 ft   4 ft

Set at one even non-jumping stride from the first element to the second, then two short strides to the third element.

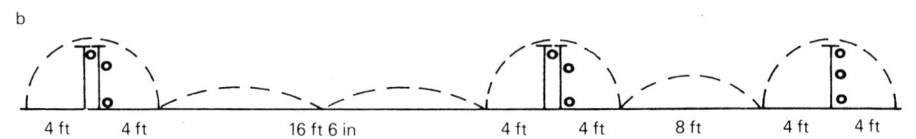

b

4 ft   4 ft   16 ft 6 in   4 ft   4 ft   8 ft   4 ft   4 ft

Set at one even non-jumping stride to the second element, then two long strides to the third element.

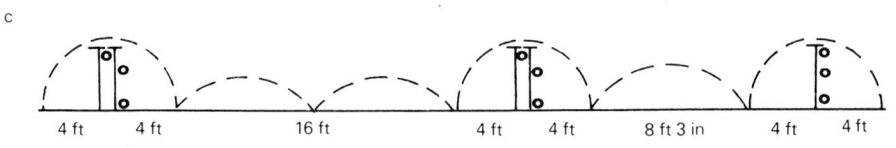

c

4 ft   4 ft   16 ft   4 ft   4 ft   8 ft 3 in   4 ft   4 ft

Set at one long non-jumping stride to the second element, then two even strides to the third element.

A typical treble combination set at a junior jumping show — running spread to vertical to vertical.

You will see from the third *Fig., 19c*, that by shortening the distance between the first and second elements we have made pony and rider contain their stride to come out over the second element. In *Fig. 19b* you will see that we have lengthened the distance in the double to force pony and rider to lengthen their stride to get one even non-jumping stride to come out over the second element. In *Figs. 20, a, b, c*, we have repeated the exercises 'long' and 'short' or 'short' and 'long' in the treble combination.

These distance exercises can be made progressively more difficult according to the type of fences used for each element of the combinations. It is easier for the rider to regulate the pony's stride if he is going into a vertical fence to a spread fence in a long-distance double combination, and going into a spread fence to a vertical in the short-distance double combination. In treble combinations a vertical, with a long distance to a spread, following by a true distance to a spread, or a spread then a long one-stride distance to a spread, followed by a true two-stride distance to a spread is the best for novice jumping ponies. So although we can 'play' with the distances to train the pony at this stage it would be unfair to 'play' with the type of fence for each element as this would be beyond the novice pony. I would not start this sort of distance exercise until the pony has had considerable experience in novice jumping classes in the show ring.

William coming through a double combination. See how he gets the one even stride in the middle.

Water Jumps

The final stage of preparation is jumping water jumps. I purposely leave this until the very last phase. Water jumps and ditches are often part of modern show jumping courses but are very rarely in novice pony classes, except perhaps a novice championship, but nevertheless they are going to have to be faced eventually.

The basis of the technique of jumping water or ditches is to see them and treat them quite simply as spread fences. There is no point in galloping at them like a racehorse in a sprint race.

I place small water troughs under a fence as early as possible on our ponys' training programmes so they get quite used to seeing water under a fence. Once they have got used to these ditches, either dry or with water in them, they do not seem to present any problems. But jumping water is an entirely different subject altogether and must be treated separately.

Start off by going back to lungeing with loose-fitting elastic side-reins and use a small water jump first. We are lucky having dykes in our area which serve the purpose beautifully. However, a small stream will do the job, or you can dig out two water jumps, one at about 4 ft in length, and the other at about 6 ft in length. Place a small brush fence, or board fence, in front of the water, and a rail (about 76 cm [2 ft 6 in] high) approximately two-thirds of the way over the water. You must have two rails leaning against the wings for the lunge rein to slip over. (*Fig. 21*). Lunge the pony on a nice big circle at the trot and then, with the encouragement of the lunge whip — just flicking it, present him to the water on a relatively short approach. The rail will encourage him to go for height, and that height will give him the length to jump the water; the rail will also discourage him from simply trotting through the water. Once this has been done successfully the pony can be worked at the canter on a longer approach to the water. We want the highest point of the pony's jump to be just over the centre of the water, so if he is not getting up into the air and making the length, raise the pole set over the water.

Now the pony can be worked under saddle, but this time we place a set of sloping rails from the front of the water to about the centre.

Stage 1

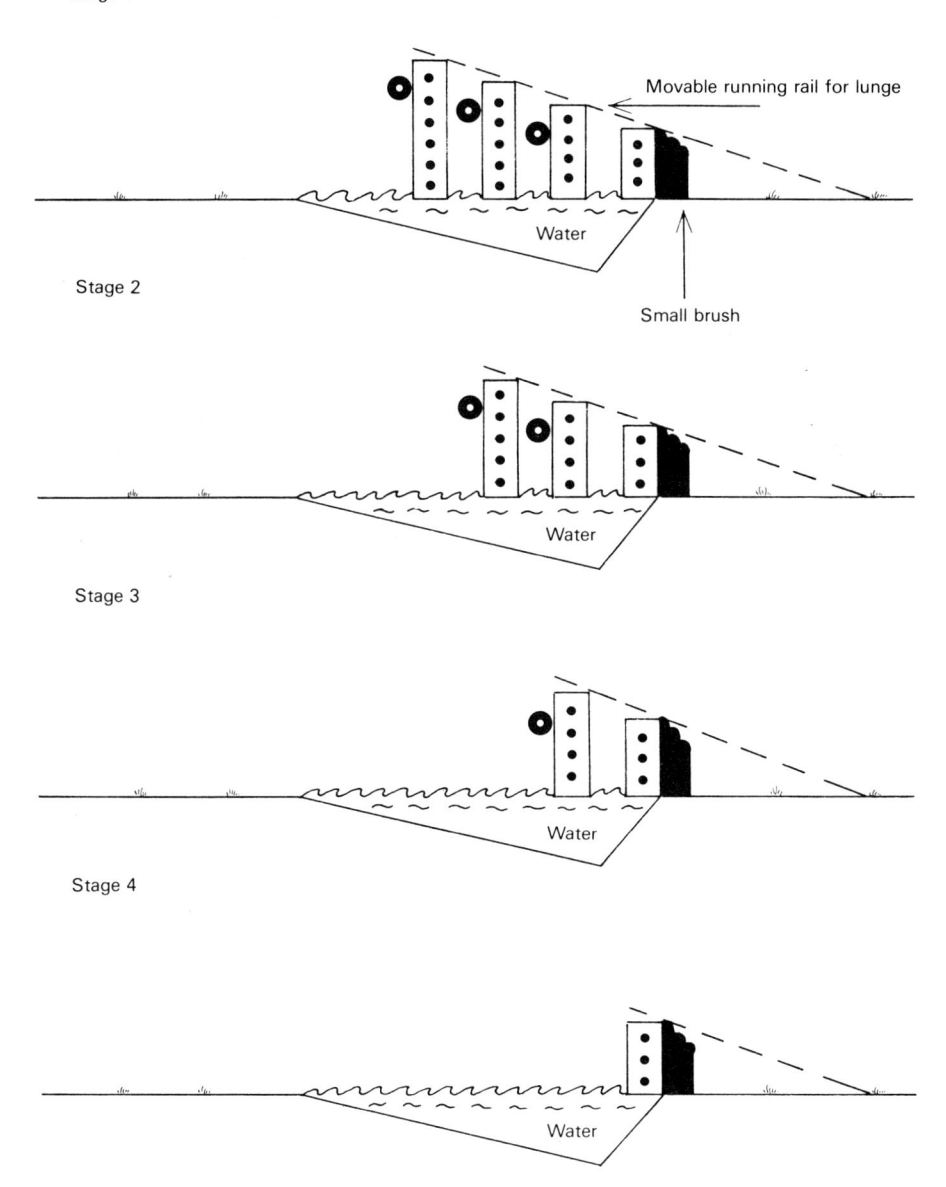

Movable running rail for lunge

Water

Stage 2

Small brush

Water

Stage 3

Water

Stage 4

Water

Fig. 21 Schooling over water on lunge and under saddle in four stages.

Water jump, with a rail set for a novice competition.

As the pony's technique improves, the top rail can be taken away, and so on, until the pony is jumping a plain water jump only, with confidence and accuracy.

We can start thinking about competition at this stage and the way we build up to this is to make at least two dummy runs close to home. On the first dummy run we go to a local equestrian centre where they hold numerous jumping shows and their facilities include an outdoor jumping arena and an indoor jumping arena. We practise under as near competition conditions as we can, over both the outdoor course and the indoor course. We spend two to three mornings at the Mill Lodge Equestrian Centre, near Wisbech, but most centre owners, like David and Janet Edgson, will hire out their facilities for schooling by the hour, morning or full day. Not only do we, of course, get valuable practice at jumping in a ring but also the short journey gets the ponies ready for travelling.

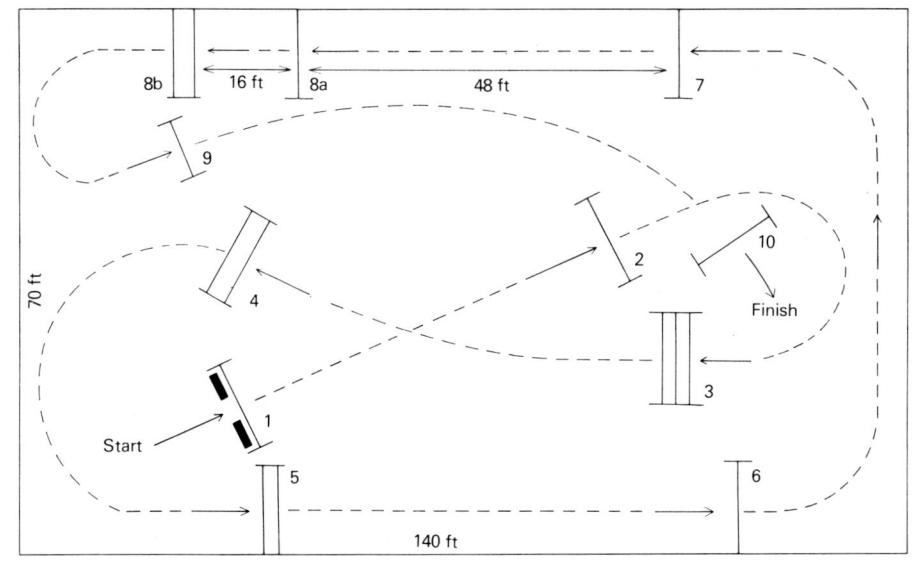

Fig. 22 Suggested layout for a schooling course.

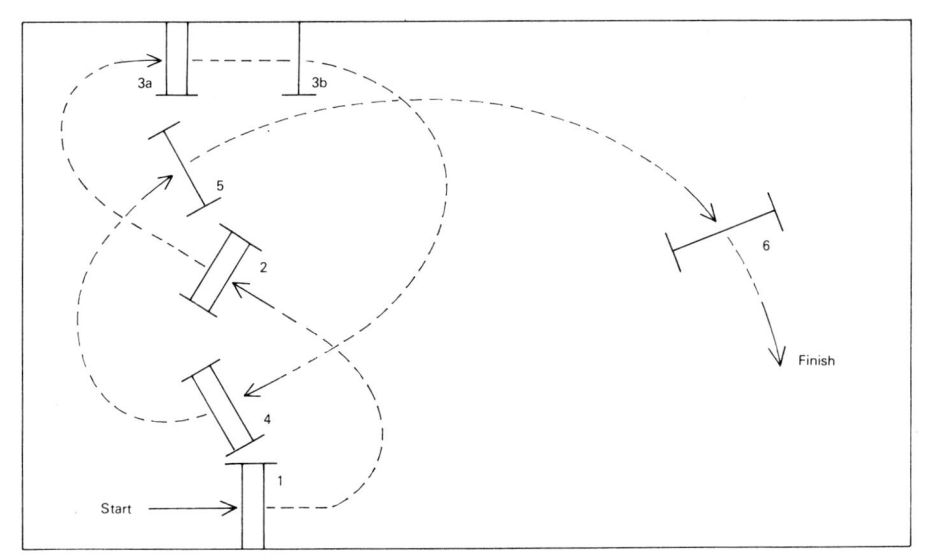

Fig. 23 Suggested layout for practising jump-off courses.

93

We follow this up with a full dress rehearsal at a proper show. Most show secretaries will allow you, if you ask nicely and pay the expenses such as for the loose-boxes etc., to take a couple of ponies to their meetings for a dummy run and we make this outing some distance away from home to simulate real competition conditions. With William and Fiddler we took them to the All Wales & West Showground in South Wales with the kind permission of Mr Fred Broome, senior. We stayed three days so that the ponies could experience and settle to the atmosphere of a showground. During the day the ponies were walked around the showground and worked in the practice rings. At the end of the last show day, we then schooled both of them over the junior show jumping courses. So when they went for their first competitive show outing we had no problems of 'over-excitement' or 'stage fright'.

For your first show it is best to pick a local, unaffiliated show, or a schooling show. In Great Britain the Riding Club shows are the best form of schooling show for the pony and rider to gain experience, and in America there are plenty of schooling shows during the winter and spring months.

One final tip before you go off to win your red rosettes. If your pony goes well in his first four to six public outings and gets into a jump-off, do not suddenly ride him against the clock. It is better, and wiser, to ride him just for another smooth, clear round. After, say, two outings in jump-offs against the clock, if all has gone well, then you can start putting him under progressive pressure on shorter routes to the finishing line to beat the clock and your rivals.

Many Riding Club and Pony Club shows now have what is called Clear Round jumping and this is a wonderful medium for warming-up a novice pony. When William and Fiddler were in their early competition days we always slipped them in the clear round jumping before they went into the main ring for their class.

7 Preparing for the show

The night beforehand, clean all your tack, your riding gear and the pony's clothing, and prepare the bandages. Check that you have plenty of spares, e.g. stirrup-leathers, reins, girths, jumping studs, etc.

Go to the stables early in the morning, muck out the pony's box and feed him. While the pony is enjoying his breakfast you and your helpers (usually the family) can be loading all the tack and gear into the motor horse-box, or trailer. Two travelling containers will be needed for the equipment, one for your pony, clothing and bandages, etc., and the other for spare items of equipment. Put in two full hay nets and enough feed for the day plus water buckets, water containers, and a medicine basket with first aid kit for both equines and humans. (Your veterinarian will advise on the items you will need in your first aid box). Also take a large torch, grooming equipment, spare plaiting-up material, and waterproof clothing for both pony and rider.

Check that the pony has eaten his feed and then tie him up. Remove the night rugs, but if it is a cold morning place a loose rug over his body. Now the name has got to be plaited, or braided. Six

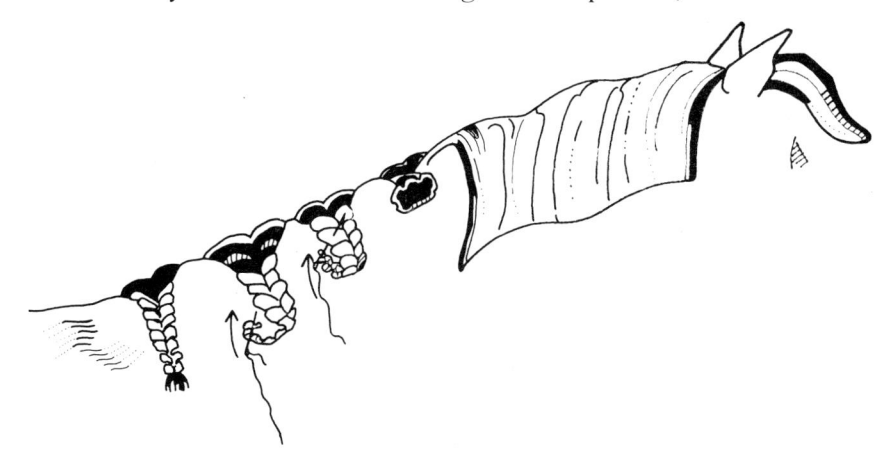

Fig. 24 Main plaiting. To finish off, double the plait under and pass the needle through the plait.

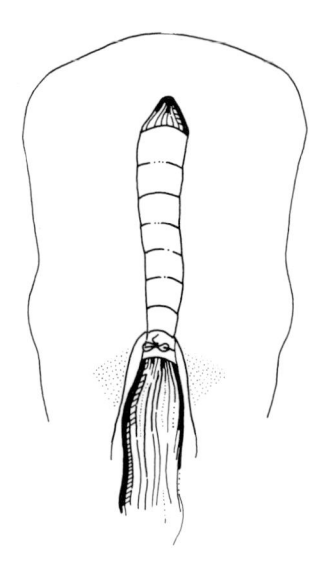

Fig. 25 Tail bandaging. Maintain a fairly tight pressure and secure the bandage by the tapes, with the tie finishing on the outside of the tail, not underneath.

plaits are required including the forelock, or any even number above this but the forelock must be included. Materials required will be: a water brush, a mane comb, a reel of strong thread (the colour of the mane, i.e. brown, black or white) a needle with a large eye and a pair of scissors.

First, cut some pieces of thread to about 20 cm (8 in) and lay them out on a clean stable rubber so that you can see them clearly. Then, wet the mane down with a water brush. Divide the mane with the mane comb into five equal parts. Start plaiting at the poll by dividing a portion of the mane into three equal strands. When about two thirds of the way down, take one the lengths of thread by its middle and begin to plait it in. On reaching the end of the plait, take the two ends of the thread and pass them around the end of the plait and pull tight. When all the plaits are done, check they are more or less of uniform length and thickness. Then take the needle, pass through its eye the two ends of the thread, double the plait under itself and pass the needle through the plait. Pull the ends of the thread through the needle, put the needle away (in your lapel or sweater), take the two ends again, bind the thread around the plait and then knot at the top of the plait. Cut any excess pieces of thread away with the scissors. The finished product should be pleasing to the eye with even and tight plaits close to the crest.

There are other methods of mane plaiting, principally the elastic band method, but this does not give such a pleasing result as the thread.

To put on the tail bandage, dampen and straighten the top hairs of the tail with a water brush. Take a bandage, unroll about 20 cm (8 in), place the left hand under the tail, holding the unrolled portion of the bandage, while the right hand holds the roll. Pass the unrolled portion under the tail with the left hand and set it at a slight upward angle. Now start turning the roll around the tail with the right hand. Make one tour and then turn over the corner of the first portion that was placed by the left hand. Continue down the tail in uniform turns and maintain a fairly tight pressure. On reaching the end, secure the bandage by the tapes and roll in the loose ends. Lift the tail away from the hocks and bend into a comfortable and straight form. When you arrive at the show remove the tail bandage by simply grasping it at the nearest point to the dock and pull it down.

Next 'quarter' the pony by giving him a light brushing, remove any overnight stains and sponge out his eyes, nostrils and dock. Then pick his feet out and grease them. Put on the travelling rug, with a blanket underneath if it is a very cold morning. At this stage the travelling bandages, or boots, can be put on all four legs. Now it is all systems go for the first serious show.

Warming up

It is difficult to generalize about the warming-up procedure at a show. Ponies and horses, like human athletes, differ enormously in the amount of warming up they need. Some need very little, others need a considerable amount of time. William, for instance, needs very little warming up but he must be kept on the move just before his turn to go into the arena then he canters straight in with his eyes sparkling, ears cocked and that 'getting down to business' look

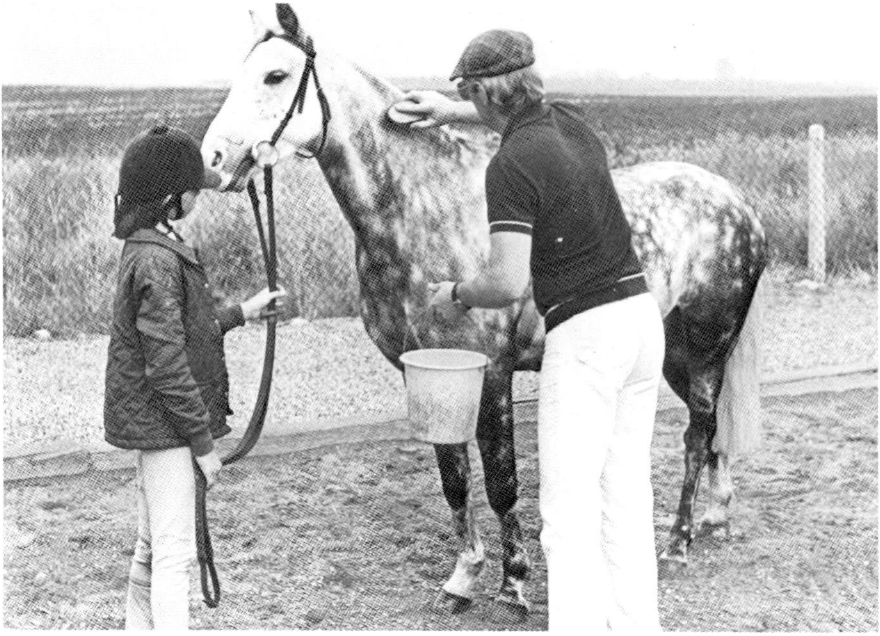

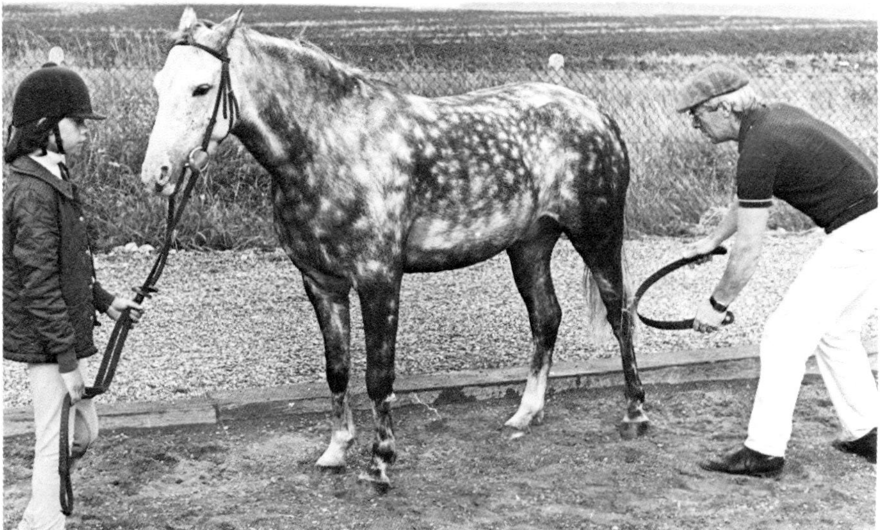

After every workout in spring and summer we wash the ponies down, including their tails. The same is carried out before and after a show.

about him. But Fiddler needs a lot of time, with plenty of flat-work, half-halting, changes of rein, circles, small and large, and several practice jumps at the trot and canter. Then he has to be allowed to think that it is all over for about ten minutes before he goes in and then is ready for action. So there is no way anyone can give hard and fast rules on warming up. But two tips I can give you, warm up well on the flat and over small fences. Then warm up over a vertical fence and a spread fence but do not try to find out how high your pony can jump in the practice ring — the arena is the place for that. And it is better to under-do your warming up than over-do it. You will soon learn just what is needed to get your pony 'right' for going into the competition ring. I have seen too many contests lost in the practice ring and not enough of them won there. So use your intelligence and experience. Don't be tempted to impress in the practice ring, that is not the place to do it.

Walking the Course

This is where things really begin to get serious. Never underestimate the value of walking the course and certainly never rush it. Allow yourself plenty of time first to study the course plan, if one is available, and then, especially, the jump-off course plan. As you walk into the arena stop for a few minutes and study the general layout. Get firmly fixed in your mind the relation between the entry to the arena and the first fence. Then plan where you are going to circle while waiting for the starting bell, or klaxon.

Often one sees riders huddled around talking, or just wandering from one fence to another, but this is not the way to walk the course and certainly not the way to win competitions. Far better to set off with your coach, or one of your parents, and start at the very beginning — the approach to the start line. Set out to walk the complete track you will be taking with your pony, working out the turns, how you are going to use the space available in the arena and the state of the ground, whether it is uphill or downhill, where the rough patches are and where the smooth patches are. Inspect each fence individually, touch them, feel them, try to get to know each one and its characteristics. Where fences are set close together, stride out the distance: you know your pony's stride, so work out how many strides you think you will need to present him at a fence well. In the double and treble combination, try to measure the inside distances by striding them from an imaginary line which you think will be the highest point of your pony's jump, to his highest point over the second, third or last element. With this information you can decide whether the double and treble are going to ride long or short. Finally, stand in the middle of the arena and talk yourself through the course, 'There's the first fence, then come on the right rein to the second, then back to the third...' and so on.

If you are not among the first to go, watch the other competitors jump so that you can judge how the course is riding. Then when it comes to your turn, get into the ring quickly, keep your pony on the move and try to canter him around the fences so that he can get some idea of where he is but don't, of course, actually 'show' him any particular fence because you can get eliminated for that.

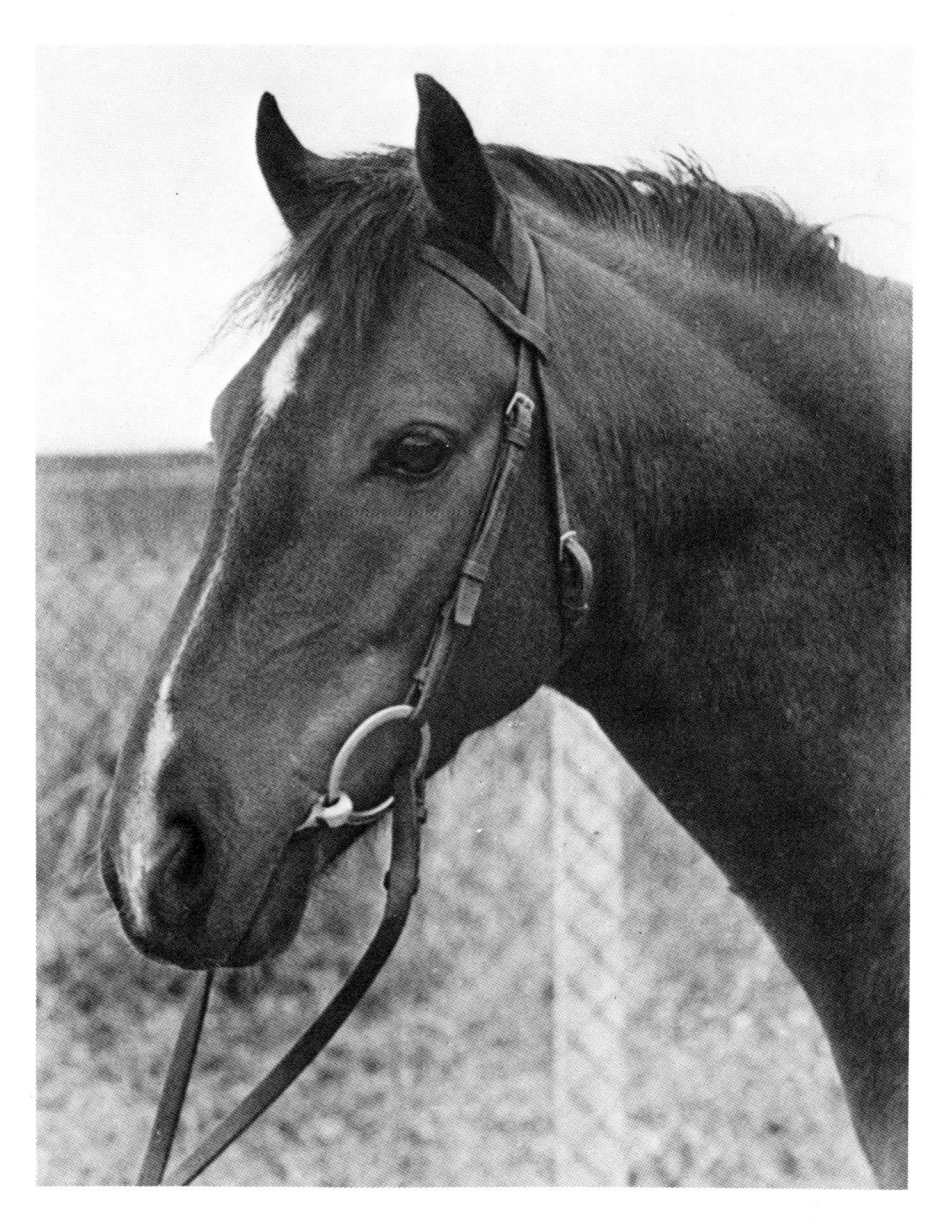

Fiddler, real name Erntold Fiddler, foaled in 1975. A 12.2 hh Welsh Section B bay gelding by Kingshead Regalia out of Hambledon Foxtrot.

William, real name Prince de Galles, foaled in 1972. A 13 hh grey gelding by Bwlch Hill Wind out of Treharne Vanessa. William is typical of the famous Welsh blood-line, Bwlch Valentino.

Back at Home

Try to arrange well in advance for somebody to prepare the loose box during the time the pony has been away so that he can come home to a warm box and clean, fresh bedding and water. Once the pony is back in his loose box, take off his tail bandage, travelling bandages and rugs. Then leave him alone for some 30 minutes to unwind and most probably to have a roll and a stale.

Come back to let his plaits down, brush him over and rug him up for the night. Put up a sweet smelling hay net and feed a gruel, or bran mash, and turn the pony loose for the night.

Later that night we like to go to the barn just to see that the ponies have settled down and eaten their feed. We check the water buckets, shake up the bedding and have a quiet inspection to see if there are any knocks or swollen joints after the day's competitions. Finally we check all bolts and ventilation and leave them to enjoy a good night's rest. We return to the house to re-live the day and have the inevitable post-mortens on performance which one always has, come win or lose.

Addy, real name Adrienne, born in Paris in 1969. Taught by her father, Peter Churchill, she started riding when she was between five and six years old, and started serious competition riding when she was ten.

8 The Care of Equipment

The equine athlete, like any other sporting performer, must have efficient equipment which is well looked after. Many a good class has been lost through the breakage of stirrup-leathers and reins; the chances of this happening can be brought to a minimum by regularly cleaning and checking all equipment. So let us go through the organization and techniques required to look after your equipment so that it will last and, above all, so that it will be safe to use.

Storage

A workshop, garage, or garden shed will serve very well as a tack room and equipment store. The bridles should be kept on a round or half-moon shaped holder so that they do not lose their shape. The best form of saddle rack is either a steel 'saddle-shaped' frame of about 46 m (18 in) in length, or a wooden frame, in a reversed V-shape, attached either to the tack room wall or to a free-standing wooden saddle horse. The stirrup leathers, irons and girths should be taken off the saddle when not in use and hung on the hook individually. This will ensure that the leathers and girths are kept in a flat shape. All martingales, if you use them, should be hung by the neck-strap.

A stable rubber makes an effective dust cover for saddles but if you can get saddle-covers so much the better.

The tack-room should be dry, with an even temperature, although leather tack should not be kept close to artificial heating.

Rugs, blankets, boots, exercise sheets, etc., can be stored in a box, trunk or basket, while leg bandages, tail bandages and so on can be kept in a drawer, or a cupboard. All these items of horse-clothing must be dry and clean before being put away or stored. If it is necessary to store tack for long periods, cover all the leather parts with a thin coating of vaseline, or neatsfoot oil. This treatment will protect the leather and keep it in good condition.

Materials needed for cleaning tack

Some form of protective overall, or apron.
A tin of saddle soap, or a bar of glycerine saddle soap.
A softening agent (i.e. vegetable oil).
Metal polish.
Two sponges: one for applying saddle soap, one for cleaning.
A duster, or soft cloth, for polishing.
Two stable rubbers: one for drying, the other to act as a dust cover.
A burnisher for irons or bits made of plain steel and some silver sand. (Very rarely used now as most items of this sort are nickel plated).
A chamois leather for drying.
A dandy brush for brushing off dirt on serge linings.
A narrow piece of wood, or something similar, for cleaning out awkward areas such as leather holes, buckles, etc.
A rubber or plastic bucket three-quarters full with luke warm water and no artifical cleaning agent added.

Cleaning the saddle

First, strip the saddle of leathers, stirrup-irons, girth buckle guards, girth, and numnah, if one is used. Place the saddle on the saddle horse. Take the irons off the leathers and place them in the bucket. Put the leathers and girth over the saddle horse. Tack cleaning time is a perfect opportunity for inspecting the equipment for any signs of wear and tear, or faults. Pay particular attention to inspecting all stitching, buckles and the girth straps.

We start with the saddle as this can then be left to dry while all the attachments are cleaned. Most modern jumping saddles are now leather lined so this can be sponged clean with a damp sponge, taking all sweat and dirt deposits away. Now the entire saddle can be sponged over and then dried with the chamois leather. The chamois should be soaked in water and then well wrung out before use.

The saddle should now be ready for soaping. Take a damp sponge and cover it fairly generously with saddle soap. Then start with the underneath, applying the soap in circular movements, but remember that tack cleaning is not just a tidying-up process, it also a way of 'feeding' the leather, so work the soap well in. Then placing the saddle on the saddle horse, repeat the process on the seat, skirt, panels, flaps and girth tabs, giving the underside of the leather, especially the flaps, a thorough coating too. The underside is more absorbant, being the flesh side of the hide, so plenty of soap will be required on the sponge. The saddle is treated with neatsfoot oil, or vegetable oil (these feed the leather and keep it soft). If any leather tack is to be stored for a long period a generous coating of either of these materials will keep it in tip-top condition. The oil is more efficiently applied with the hands. When all is done, place the saddle on the saddle rack and cover with a stable rubber or a dust cover.

Numnahs

Numnahs are made of sheepskin or felt — brush well or wash. Make sure they are well dried and aired before use.

Girths

Attention must be given to the condition of the girth when cleaning, no matter what material it is made of. The girth is the rider's lifeline so any defects such as fraying, broken strands on string or nylon girths, splits or cracks on webbing or leather girths, must be attended to immediately. The best treatment for a worn or damaged girth is to throw it away. The stitching at the buckles is another danger point but this can be repaired by a saddler. A girth in poor condition, or one that has been neglected, can seriously injure the pony. Girth galls, sore elbows or sore ribs will result and these are not ailments which will clear up quickly when the horse or pony is in serious training.

Leather Girths Clean and soap in the same way as the saddle. Clean the buckles. For the 'folded' type of leather girth it is worth treating the inside of the folds with neatsfoot oil to keep the girth soft. After cleaning, hang all girths up by the buckles to keep them in good shape.

Web, string and nylon girths These should be brushed daily but they do have a tendency to go hard, so washing with pure soap (flakes or liquid) will be necassary at least once a week. They must be completely dry before re-use. Be careful with some string and nylon girths as these have been known to shrink. Coloured girths will in some cases lose a certain amount of their colour when washed.

Stirrups

Leathers Wash carefully and then soap. At the same time check that the stitching is in good order and for signs of wear and tear in the leather. Many a good show jumping class has been lost by a broken stirrup leather! Clean the buckles and finally see that all holes are free of soap, oil or dirt deposits. To store, hang up by the buckles.

Irons Wash in the bucket and then dry with a stable rubber, or soft cloth. See that the 'eye' of the iron is clean and that it is not misshapen or worn thin. Too much play between the leather and the area of the 'eye' can be dangerous. Rubber treads that fit into the base of the irons have become an essential item of any jumping rider's equipment. Their aim is to help the rider to keep the ball of his foot on the iron, leaving his heels and ankles free to give support and balance to his seat. These rubber-treads should be removed from the iron and washed.

The Bridle

Periodically, about once a month, bridles should be taken to pieces completely and each part thoroughly sponged clean before being given a generous coating of neatsfoot oil or saddle soap. This is also a good time for checking on the condition of the bridle and bit.

For daily cleaning it is not necessary to take the bridle apart completely. Just take the noseband off, drop the cheekpieces down to the last hole, and place the mouthpieces only in the bucket of lukewarm water and wash. Next wipe the headpiece clean with a damp sponge and hang the bridle on a hook, or over the end of a saddle rack. Now with the damp sponge wipe the rest of the bridle clean. The sponge can be curled over so that both sides of the leather are cleaned at the same time. Sponge the reins, starting at the union with the mouthpiece and pulling the sponge all the way down to the buckle. Reins can vary considerably these days according to personal taste; plain leather, plaited leather, nylon and rubber-covered (which are the type we use), so your cleaning technique will depend on the type you have and the material they are made of. Next sponge the browband clean and then the noseband. The complete bridle can now be dried with the chamois leather and the saddle soap applied, treating both the inside and outside of the leather. Dry and polish the mouthpiece with a soft cloth, or a stable rubber, but don't use metal polish. Then with the narrow piece of wood (a nail should not be used as it can damage the leather) clear all dirt deposits from the moving parts of the mouthpiece and free the holes and keepers of the bridle from soap and/or water deposits. Finally, put the noseband back on the bridle, adjust all buckles to their original fittings and hang the bridle up on a bridle rack.

Horse clothing

All rugs, night and day versions, paddock sheets, exercise quarter-sheets, etc., must be cleaned regularly. From time to time they should be washed or dry-cleaned. Summer sheets and rugs, for example, should be cleaned around the end of October before being stored for the winter months, and winter clothing should be dry-cleaned or washed around mid-April before being stored for the summer months. Preventive measures must be taken to guard against moths and damp during storage.

Other items

Modern materials now used for the making and design of jumping boots and overeach boots, etc., have simplified cleaning techniques and care to a basic minimum of just washing and/or brushing.

Care of practice fences and schooling area

This is one area of maintenance that is often neglected but is nonetheless an essential part of the efficiency of any modern show jumping yard. The main points of advice I would like to give here are: keep your jumping rails, fillers and wings, bright and clean; if the paintwork gets chipped or faded then take a day off from the intense atmosphere or schooling and enjoy yourself with some pots of paint and brushes. Check for any cracks or splits appearing in the jumping rails; if you catch this type of wear and tear early the rail can be 'banded' but if the damage has weakened the rail it is wiser to replace it. The schooling arena, whether it be a wood-bark, sand, tan or grass surface will need a daily raking. With a grass surface a disc-harrow and/or a Cambridge (ridged) roller should be used about twice a week.

Jumping studs

Anti-slip heel studs (jumping studs) should be fitted to jumpers when they are asked to perform on poor or wet surfaces. It is necessary, therefore, to have shoes fitted that are specially designed for the studs. These shoes have a thread-hole at each heel, either two or one according to the type of stud to be used. The studs are fitted by screwing them into these holes, but when the studs are not used the stud-holes should be packed with cotton wool to protect the thread and to keep dirt particles out of the holes.

Caroline Bradley riding Tigre at the Birmingham International Show.

Malcolm Pyrah riding Towerlands Anglezarke at Hickstead.

Glossary

AIDS   A system of signals by which the rider controls the pony. Natural aids are hands, legs, seat and voice, unnatural aids are whip, spurs and martingales, etc.

BALANCE   A pony is said to be balanced when his weight and that of his rider are so distributed as to allow him to use himself with maximum ease and efficiency.

BIT   The mouthpiece of a bridle.

CADENCE   Term defining the rhythm and evenness of a pony's stride.

COLLECTION   The concentration of the pony's energy occurring when the body is collected into a shortened form and is ready to obey the rider's aids instantly.

COMBINATIONS   Two or more fences so spaced that for competition purposes they are judged as one obstacle. These can be double, treble or quadruple combinations. If a pony runs out or refuses between or at any element, the competitor must return to the first element and jump the complete combination again. Faults incurred at each element are totalled together by the judges.

FOREHEAD   Area of the pony's body in front of the saddle.

HAND   Unit for measuring the height of a horse or pony in the UK, equal to 10 cm (4 in).

HEAD COLLAR   Made of leather for handling an unbridled horse or pony. (In America often described as Head Stall).

IMPULSION   The forward energy created by active hocks.

INDEPENDENT SEAT   A rider is said to have an independent seat when his balance, position and security in the saddle is not reliant on the reins or stirrup-irons.

LOOSE BOX   Stabling for horse and pony where the animal is left loose. Average size about 3 m (12 ft) square.

LUNGE REIN   Long webbing rein measuring about 7.6 m (25 ft).

MARTINGALE   An artificial aid designed to prevent the pony from holding his head above the angle of control.

NEAR SIDE   Left side.

NUMNAH   A felt or sheepskin pad placed under the saddle.

OFF SIDE   Right Side.

OXER   Obstacle formed with rails and a brush or hedge fence.

REIN BACK   The walk backwards when the pony moves regularly in two-time with the hindlegs remaining well in line.

RISING TROT   When the rider rises up and down in the saddle at the trot, known as 'posting' in America.

SEAT   The rider's position in the saddle. Can also mean one of the natural aids which controls pace and impulsion.

TACK   Term used to describe saddlery equipment.

TRANSITION   A change of pace and speed.

TWO-TRACK   When the hindlegs follow a separate track, to one side or other of the track being made by the forelegs.

Simplified Rules of Show Jumping

Under British Show Jumping Association Rules:

1. There are no marks or faults for style.
2. Each fence is judged separately.
3. Knocking down a fence — 4 faults.
4. Refusals: first, 3 faults; second, 6 faults; third, elmination. Refusals are cumulative and the third refusal in the complete round eliminates the competitor.
5. Fall of Pony or Rider — 8 faults.
6. Time: The course has to be completed within the time allowed which is based on the number of yards per minute required by the conditions of the competition. Exceeding the time allowed is penalized at the rate of a ¼ fault for every second or part of a second. The time limit is double the time allowed. Exceeding the time limit is penalized by elimination.
7. Where there is a jump-off of competitors on equal scores, the rider with the fastest time and the least faults is the winner.

Useful Addresses

AMERICAN HORSE SHOWS ASSOCIATION, 527, Madison Avenue, New York. N.Y. USA.

BRITISH EQUESTRIAN FEDERATION, British Equestrian Centre, Kenilworth, Warwickshire CV8 2LR, England.

BRITISH SHOW JUMPING ASSOCIATION, British Equestrian Centre, Kenilworth, Warwickshire CV8 2LR, England.

EQUESTRIAN FEDERATION OF AUSTRALIA, Royal Showground, Epsom Road, Ascot Vale, 3032 Australia.

THE PONY CLUB OF GREAT BRITAIN, British Equestrian Centre, Kenilworth, Warwickshire CV8 2LR, England.

US PONY CLUBS, 303 South High Street, West Chester, Pennsylvania, USA. 19380.

Acknowledgements

I would like to thank the following for their goodwill and co-operation: Janet and David Edgson of the Mill Lodge Equestrian Centre, Elaine and Peter Kemp of the Blackborough End Riding School, and Leslie Lane, equestrian photographer.

Peter Churchill
South Eau Farm, 1981

Picture Credits

The photographs on pages 20, 22, 77, 111 and 112 are by Steve Yarnell. All the other photographs are Leslie Lane's. The line art work was drawn by Christine Taylor.

Index

Athletic ability of pony 15-19
   training 35-37

Balance 38-41
Bandage, tail 97
Behaviour, natural 11
   trained 11
Bitting 76-77
Bradley, Caroline 111
Broome, David 77
Broome, Fred, sen. 9, 37, 78
Boots, brushing 32
   jumping 32
   over-reach 32

Cannon 16
Canter, leading leg 47-49
Cavalletti 59
Chest 17
Chute jumping 31
Circle work 55-58
Clothing, horse 109
Collection 38-41
Condition, lack of 79

Distance(s), even 86-88
   long 86-88
   problems 86-88
   short 86-88
Dunning, Pam 22

Equipment 32
   care of 105-110
Exercise, three-fence 84-85

Exercising 35-37

Feet 15
Fences, care of 109-110
   practice 29-30, 82-93
   refusing at 74-75
   running out at 76
   rushing 74
Fletcher, Graham 20
Forearm 16

Girth 17, 107-8

Half-halt 53-54
Haunches-in 53-54
Head 18
Hocks 16

Jumping box 31
   lane 31, 81-82

Lungeing 59-64, 66-68

Mane plaiting 95-97

Neck 18

Pastern 16
Physical rider 8-9
Points of the pony 13
Presentation 78
Pyrah, Malcolm 112

Quartering 97

Rein-back 115
Rein(s), draw- 33, 42
  elastic side- 33, 61
  lunge- 59-64
Rhythm 41-43
Rules, show jumping 115

Schooling, free-style 69-70
  stick 66
Shoulder 16
  -in 50-51
Smith, Harvey 77
Spurs 42
Studs, jumping 110

Tack, bad fitting 76-77

  cleaning 106-109
Tail 17
Technical rider 8-9
Tendons 16
Training 37-38
  area 26-27
  lack of 78
Transitions 45-47
Turn on the forehand 49-50

Uncollected 39-40

Walking the course 100
Warming up 97-99
Water jumps 90-92
Welch, Freddie 18